INTERNATIONAL CURRENCY ARRANGEMENTS AND POLICIES

INTERNATIONAL CURRENCY ARRANGEMENTS AND POLICIES

JULIUS HORVATH

Nova Science Publishers, Inc.
New York

For permission to use material from this book please contact us:
Telephone 631-231-7269; Fax 631-231-8175
Web Site: http://www.novapublishers.com

Library of Congress Cataloging-in-Publication Data
Available upon request.

ISBN 1-60021-226-3

Published by Nova Science Publishers, Inc. ✦New York

CONTENTS

INTRODUCTION

This book deals with exchange rate arrangements and exchange rate policies.

Chapter 1 classifies exchange rates into flexible, intermediate and rigid arrangements. We then subdivide these arrangements into free float, managed float, pegged but adjustable, target zone, crawling peg, hard peg, currency board, dollarization, and monetary union. This chapter also discusses hypothesis of vanishing intermediate exchange rate arrangements as well as it deals with differentiation between de jure, and de facto exchange rate arrangements.

Chapter 2 deals with issue of choosing an appropriate exchange rate arrangement. We briefly characterize basic approaches of how to choose exchange rate regime. Furthermore, we in a more detailed manner review considerations stemming from the optimum currency area literature.

Chapter 3 deals with problems of exchange rate, which were encountered by the most developed transition countries. After discussing the initial stabilization problems of the early 1990s we provide a general overview of the macroeconomic situation and exchange rate arrangements in these countries in the period 1990-2004. Also we discuss issues connected with future introduction of euro into these countries.

Chapter 4 provides the reader with two case studies. First, we discuss the Czech experience in the transition period till the crisis in May 1997. Second, we discuss Hungarian experience concerning banking and exchange rate policy in the 1990s till the early years of this century.

Chapter 1

EXCHANGE RATE ARRANGEMENTS

Cohen (1998) contends that there are different reasons, which lead countries to introduce their own currency as a legal tender. Among these reasons political symbolism, right to seignorage, and exploiting currency in managing the economy seem to be the most important.

Currency is a political symbol. It is difficult to evaluate the strength of populations' attachment to national currency, particularly as compared to other national symbols as sport-team or national anthem. However, it seems – at least in some countries – that currency as a political symbol promotes a sense of collectivity among different groups in the society. For example, after the break-up of the former socialist countries as the Soviet Union, Yugoslavia and Czechoslovakia, new countries had emerged and re-emerged on the world political map. All of these new countries have introduced their own currency, i.e. the Soviet ruble, the Yugoslavian dinar or the Czechoslovak koruna did not survive the collapse of the state (political regime) it had created them. To a certain extent similar process was seen after the break-up of large colonial entities into sovereign states in the 1960s. This sends a signal that the notion of national money is still inseparable from the idea of sovereign statehood. National money provides governments with the possibility to avoid dependence on other country. A country, which wants real political autonomy cannot count on someone else' money. On the other hand we observe that separation of national money from national states is occurring. Some, especially, the European countries join monetary union, i.e. they give up national money. But also countries consider - in an increasing extent - possibility to dollarize, i.e. to introduce foreign currency as a domestic legal tender. Furthermore, competition across borders transforms the role of the state in monetary affairs. States remain influential through jurisdiction over the supply of national money, but the demand side (the willingness of population to hold this money) is slowly changing which leads states to function more as oligopolist not as monopolist in this respect.

Seignorage is an important source of revenue for the state, which stems from the function of the state as issuer of the currency. There are different definitions of seignorage, among them the simplest one considers seignorage as the excess of the nominal value of a currency over its cost of production. It is also a less costly way of taxing the public, and under circumstances of high economic and political instability, as a sudden crisis, it gives an exceptional weapon into the hands of the government.

Macroeconomic considerations are also important when sovereign countries stick to their currency. Typically people do not believe in 'policy ineffectiveness proposition', i.e. that economic policy does not matter, quite to the opposite people believe in potentially positive or negative effects of monetary and exchange rate policies. It is believed that monetary and exchange rate policy affects – at least in the short run - domestic real economic variables and thus provides a source of power to those who control these policies. For example, by influencing the level and the change of money supply not only domestic resident expenditures can be affected but also the trade-off between unemployment and the inflation, again to the extent that such trade-off exists. The exact structures through which monetary and exchange rate policy affects real variables are not exactly known, which not only generates uncertainty but also opens the possibility of mismanaging monetary affairs.

Exchange rate management has its macroeconomic and microeconomic dimensions. The macro dimension emphasizes the importance of establishing a credible anchor with the aim to domestic price level stability, and sees its effects in the short-run stabilization policy as well as policy discipline concerning the long-run avoidance of inflation. The micro dimension stresses the competitiveness of the economy and issues related to the efficiency of resource allocation; Guitian (1994).

Having own currency leaves the domestic policy makers with an option of deciding the arrangement in which this currency works. Policy makers make their decision based on domestic and international considerations. Typically, they consider the extent of currency flexibility guaranteed by the respective exchange rate arrangement. We point to three important issues in this respect.

First, contrast between rigid and flexible exchange rate arrangements is useful but it simplifies the problem by narrowing the choices only to this dichotomy. It is more useful to think that the flexibility of the exchange rate arrangement is a continuum where on the poles one finds fully flexible and fully rigid arrangements, and between the poles variety of different arrangements is possible.

Second, while in principle there is a ground for a belief that unregulated markets work better than regulated markets one should not apply this reasoning to the exchange rates markets in such a way, which would put very close analogy between fixed exchange rates and price controls. Niehans (1984) and Cooper (1999) argue that Johnson (1973) was of such opinion. Niehans (1984) writes that it is fallacious to think that efficiency would require clearing of the foreign exchange market by flexible exchange rate regime, "it is fallacious because market-clearing exchange rates can also be achieved under fixed rates by supplying the appropriate amount of money." (p. 286). If the money prices of all goods were perfectly flexible, then all markets would clear under peg as well as under float. In reality, prices of many goods are not flexible, however that does not imply that fixed rates prevent the occurrence of market clearing.

Third, the analogy between floating rates and free markets does not seem to hold either. Currency is not a typical commodity. It is rather an asset than a good. When exchange rates are not fixed, a crucial role is played either by legal restrictions on asset holdings or by anticipated government intervention. Modern fiat currency is un-backed and is cost-less to produce. One cannot allow a free entry into the supply of fiat currency. For most goods, supplies and demands can be determined in a free market; for fiat currencies supplies must be regulated; Wallace (1979).

Classification of Exchange Rate Arrangements

We divide exchange rate arrangements into three main clusters: flexible, intermediate, and rigid exchange rate arrangements.

Flexible Exchange Rate Arrangements

Free Float

Free float is a fully flexible exchange rate arrangement, which is characterized by no intervention by the monetary authorities in the foreign exchange rate market. This means monetary authorities do not influence behavior of exchange rate in any way, i.e. currency can strengthen or weaken to any extent without explicit or implicit intervention of the monetary authorities.

Interventions in the foreign exchange market are not the only channel through which monetary authorities influence behavior of domestic currency. For example, interest rate policy may influence exchange rate behavior, too.

An important advantage of the fully flexible exchange rate regime is that it does not require large amount of international reserves to defend the level of the currency and that the central bank and the domestic government undertakes no explicit or implicit external commitment. One can see fully flexible exchange rate regime as consistent with different monetary policy approaches, i.e. with monetary and interest rate targets, or with inflation targeting. In this respect, flexible exchange rate arrangement allows the monetary policy to concentrate on domestic considerations.

Managed Float

One can think about managed float as a continuum of options in which policy maker leaves to the market to determine the level of exchange rate, however to a certain extent explicitly or implicitly influences its value. Gandolfo (1995, p.25) recognizes an 'almost pure float', i.e. an exchange rate regime in which an "official intervention may be limited to smoothing out exchange-rate movements." In this exchange rate arrangement 'almost pure float' will be on the one end of the spectrum with 'tightly managed float' – sometimes practically indistinguishable from pegged arrangement - on the other end.

Bubula and Otker-Robe (2002) define tightly managed float as 'where authorities heavily monitor and control exchange rate movements without any commitment to a predetermined target path, but attempt to keep the exchange rate path stable.' (p.4). Gandolfo (1995, p. 25) defines this exchange rate arrangement as such in which "monetary authorities may pursue a very active intervention policy with the aim of driving the exchange rate towards what they consider an appropriate value."

In managed float no official parity or rule is determined which the authorities are to follow.

Intermediate Exchange Rate Arrangements

We include into intermediate (limited flexibility) exchange rate arrangements pegged but adjustable regimes, basket pegs, and different variants of crawling pegs, and target zones. Borders between intermediate and flexible (or rigid) arrangements are fuzzy. For example Bubula and Otker-Robe (2002) classify into intermediate exchange rates soft pegs (conventional fixed and crawling pegs and horizontal and crawling bands, which is similar to our classification) but also tightly managed floats, and hard pegs, which in our classification belong to different arrangements.

Pegged but Adjustable Exchange Rate

In this exchange rate regime currency is pegged to an 'anchor' currency or to a basket of currencies. This regime was practiced under the Bretton Woods system when a country declared parity in terms of gold (±1%) with the possibility of adjustment in case of fundamental disequilibrium. This declared possibility of adjustment makes this a soft arrangement, as Niehans (1984, p. 296) puts it "the curse of the adjustable peg is currency speculation." Specifically, under this regime speculation – once it happens – is typically 'one way street'.

Target Zones

Target zone is an exchange rate arrangement in which central parity is fixed with a band around it. Target zone differs from a peg that it allows a movement of the currency around central parity and within given bands. The appeal of target zones is that it allows flexibility, i.e. within the band the exchange rate moves when the edge of the band is reached further movement is blocked by central bank.

Krugman (1991) established theoretical comparison of the pure float with a target zone. He criticized the intuitive view that in the target zone the exchange rate behaves as under pure float until the currency is close or hits the edge of the band, whereupon the regime switches to a version of a fixed regime. Krugman showed that the pure existence of a band around the parity has an affect on the behavior of the exchange rate even if the central bank is not defending the currency and even if the currency is inside the band. In the following we explain Krugman's argument.

Assume the log exchange rate at time t, s_t, depends linearly on an aggregate 'fundamental,' f_t, and the expected change in value, E(ds)/dt. Thus,

$$s_t = f_t + \gamma\, E(ds/dt)$$

where E is the expectation operator and (ds/dt) is the change in time of the exchange rate, and γ is a parameter, and subscript t describes the time period. The fundamentals are assumed to consist of two components, a stochastic shock, v, and a variable, m, which represents any variable influenced by the central bank policy. Thus, the exchange rate changes to:

$$s_t = v_t + m_t + \gamma E(ds/dt)$$

Also, $\underline{s} < s_t < \overline{s}$ where $\underline{s}$ and $\overline{s}$ are the lower and upper edges of the exchange rate band.

Krugman's target zone model has two critical assumptions: the exchange rate target is perfectly credible, and no intervention occurs when the currency is in the interior of the exchange rate band. When the exchange rate reaches the weak edge of the band, the money supply is reduced (by an infinitesimal amount) to prevent the currency from weakening further, and vice versa.

Assume v follows a random walk. Does it follow that there is no predictable change in the exchange rate, i.e. $E(ds/dt) = 0$? In other words, the exchange rate might simply be expected to equal $v+m$ inside the band, i.e. to behave as a pure float. Krugman (1991) argues that when the currency is very close to the top of the band, a fall in v will reduce s more than a rise in v will increase s. Consequently, $E(ds/dt) < 0$, and the relationship between v and s will not be linear. If this holds when we are close to the edge of the band it would be true also when we move inside the band. Expectations will be changed and the relationship between $(v+m)$ and s will take a particular, non-linear shape. The main result in this model is that a perfectly credible target zone is inherently stabilizing: the expectations of future interventions to stabilize the exchange rate make the exchange rate more stable than the underlying fundamentals.

Crawling Peg

Crawling peg arrangement is sometimes also called shiftable parities, sliding parities and gliding parities arrangement. Niehans (1984) records that crawling peg arrangements were originally suggested by Harrod and first applied in Chile in 1965. In crawling peg regime exchange rate adjusts frequently but in relatively small steps. In this regime un-expected parity changes are replaced by gradual – typically small and pre-announced - changes of parity. Typically parity changes compare to a single or basket of currencies in some relationship to inflation differentials.

Crawling peg may appear in different variants. For example, parity can change at the discretion of central bank, or the change happens only if some indicators reach certain levels; Gandolfo (1995, p 24).

Rigid Exchange Rate Arrangements

Into rigid exchange rate arrangements we include hard peg, currency board, official dollarization and monetary (currency) union. Bubula and Otker-Robe (2002, p.4) classify into the rigid exchange rate regimes only regimes with another currency as legal tender, currency unions and currency boards, i.e. in their classification hard peg belongs to the intermediate exchange rate regimes.

All rigid exchange rate arrangements lead to a monetary policy, which is to a large extent determined.

Hard Peg

Hard peg, sometimes also called 'an immutable fixed rate' is an exchange rate regime in which the value of domestic currency in terms of some reference currency "does not vary, or varies only within narrow, predefined limits." Ghosh, Gulde Wolf (2002, p. 39). In this regime exchange rate does not move, or moves very little, while international reserves of the central bank or other instruments of monetary policy are allowed to fluctuate.

Hard peg arrangement includes the gold standard in which domestic as well as foreign currency has an exactly determined and fixed gold content. "In this case the exchange rate between any two currencies is automatically and rigidly fixed by the ratio between the gold content of the two currencies (which is called the mint parity). Gandolfo (1995, p. 21). Gandolfo (1995) differentiates between gold standard, gold exchange standard (here convertibility into gold is limited) and pure exchange standard (here convertibility into gold is completely eliminated, however the value of currencies is fixed in relation to gold). All three systems belong to hard peg exchange rate arrangements since in what they differ (the readiness of conversion of foreign exchange into gold) does not affect the extent of flexibility on which this classification is founded.

In fiat currency regime hard peg arrangements might enter into periods in which confidence in them weakens. The credibility of the hard peg can never be absolute i.e. there is always a possibility of devaluation or revaluation.

In this regime the central bank has a formal commitment to sustain the parity with clear implications on the domestic monetary policy. In other words, the hard peg narrows the scope for domestic monetary policy since the interest rate is to a large extent determined by the monetary policy of the foreign (anchor) country to which the domestic currency is pegged.

Currency Boards

We distinguish between two main forms of currency board arrangements: the currency board proper, as it was in use in the former colonial empires, and its modern version as it is used – from the early 1990s onwards - in various countries across the globe.

The main characteristic of the proper (orthodox) currency board system is that the board stands ready to exchange local currency for the foreign currency at a given fixed rate. As Walters (1989) contends orthodox currency board has no responsibility for ensuring that bank deposits are convertible into currency board notes, this is the responsibility of commercial banks. So the proper currency board converts domestic (anchor) currency for anchor (domestic) currency but does not convert deposit or assets for currency.

A proper currency boards has no discretionary power, i.e. it is only a passive institution whose operation is constrained by strict rules. This means that the proper currency board does not lend to domestic government, business and banks. Under a strict currency-board regime, interest rates adjust automatically. If investors want to switch out of domestic currency into anchor currency then the supply of domestic currency shrinks. This causes interest rates to rise, until eventually it becomes attractive for investors to hold domestic currency again.

In a proper currency board system with a banking system in work, the monetary base is fully covered by the foreign reserves however broader measures of the money supply are not covered to the full extent.

In a theoretical example of currency board and no banking system, and no capital flows, only trade can earn foreign currency. A current account surplus then means an inflow of foreign reserve currency and an increase in the money supply. In a more realistic world with bank deposits and capital flows reflecting trade flows, there would be some proportional relation between the domestic money and the foreign exchange reserves. However, in a situation in which capital flows do not originate in trade flows this proportionality disappears.

As Walters (1989, p.111) remarks the limit to potential dis-proportionality will be set by the judgment of bankers and businessmen.

The principle of the currency board was first codified in the United Kingdom in the Bank Charter Act of 1844. Currency board was to earn seignorage to colonies in addition it was to de-politicize the colonial monetary system, leaving the monetary responsibility in the hands of the colonial center. The first currency board was established in the British Mauritius in 1849; also later there were currency boards in West and East Africa, i.e. West African Currency Board, and an East African Currency Board, respectively. But there were currency boards also outside colonies, as the example of Danzig in the 1920s or Ireland from 1928 till 1943 documents. When former colonies gained independence most of them replaced currency board arrangements with own central banks, since the prevailing opinion was – at that time - that monetary dependence might be inconsistent with newly won political independence. After colonial world collapse only Singapore, Brunei, Djibouti, British territories of Bermuda, the Cayman Islands, the Falkland Islands, and Gibraltar, used orthodox or more or less orthodox currency board system; Walters (1989).

The Hong Kong currency board is a special arrangement, which deserves a short description. The currency system of Hong Kong was based on silver standard till 1934. In 1935 Hong Kong enacted the Exchange Fund Ordinance and purchased all privately held silver coins, also the note-issuing private banks had to deposit their silver reserves with this Exchange Fund and received Certificates of Indebtedness in return. The Exchange Fund sold the silver in London for sterling. From then on, if an authorized bank wanted to issue more notes, it was obligated to purchase more Certificates of Indebtedness from the Exchange Fund with sterling at a fixed rate. The peg to sterling lasted for more than three decades. In 1967 after the devaluation of the sterling it could not be sustained. Free float reigned from 1974 to 1983, but still authorized banks had to purchase Certificates of Indebtedness from the Exchange Fund if they wanted to issue more notes. But banks could borrow foreign exchange to obtain liquid assets from abroad. The start of the Sino-British negotiations over the future of Hong Kong in 1982 led to a series of financial crises. In October 1983 the government decided to go back to the currency board system again. Bank issuing notes had to purchase Certificates of Indebtedness now with US$ at fixed rate from the Exchange Fund; Kwan and Lui (1996).

Modern revival of currency boards is connected with Argentina, which introduced currency board in 1991. Later Estonia, Bulgaria, Bosnia and other countries followed example of Argentina.

Bulgaria has introduced currency board in 1997. In late 1996, Bulgaria entered a hyperinflation period. This was to a large extent caused by irresponsible government policy, which included liquidity injection to support weakening banking system, and central bank financing of the budget deficit. In late September 1996, the Bulgarian National Bank closed about one third of the Bulgarian banking sector. In June 1997 Parliament introduced a law on currency, which fixed the value of one thousand levs to one German mark; Gulde (1999).

In a modern environment introduction of the currency board serves to enhance credibility of domestic policy makers. However, the central bank - while constrained by currency board rules - still exercises considerable discretionary power. As reserves currency board holds interest-bearing assets denominated in the anchor currency, and generates seigniorage from the difference between the interest earned on its reserve assets and the expense of maintaining its liabilities in circulation. A modern currency board makes managing capital flows much harder since the central bank is not allowed to sterilize the effects of these flows on the monetary base.

Modern currency boards cannot prevent an attack on the domestic currency. The value of domestic financial assets that may be used to buy foreign currency is larger than the monetary base backed by currency reserves. On the other hand, currency board arrangement by increasing the credibility of central bankers may serve as a deterrent to such an attack.

Dollarization

Under the currency board regime the domestic country keeps its own currency and thus to a certain extent still conforms to some national sentiments and gains seignorage. This is not the case under official dollarization, which is an exchange rate arrangement in which sovereign country has no own legal tender, i.e. domestic country adopts another country's currency as a legal tender. Since this currency typically is (was) American dollar the term dollarization is used even when domestic country adopts other currency than dollar. However, the term euroization also begins to be used.

The term dollarization also describes a portfolio shift away from domestic to foreign currency, which may occur as a reaction to unstable macroeconomic conditions, but also as a rational tendency to diversify assets. Thus we need to distinguish this type of 'unoficial' dollarization, which reflects shift in preferences from "official" dollarization under which country adopts foreign currency as a legal tender.

Official dollarization can be bilaterally negotiated or done unilaterally. Only a relatively small number of countries (independent nations and dependencies) have officially adopted a foreign currency as legal tender. As of 1999 Bogetic (2000) have identified 28 countries and territories with officially dollarized economies; all are small, and many are islands, often with only a few thousand inhabitants. Six are members of the International Monetary Fund: Kiribati, the Marshall Islands, Micronesia, Palau, Panama, and San Marino. Most dollarized countries give the full legal tender status only to one foreign currency, but also cases of two simultaneous legal tenders are known; Bogetic (2000).

Much like countries operating currency board regimes, officially dollarized economies do not exercise independent monetary policies. Under both regimes, the economy adjusts to external shocks through factor and product markets with the help of the financial system.

There was an increase in dollarization type of arrangements in the 1990s. In difference to previous decades when much of the exchange rate related debates centered on the role of inflation-stabilization programs, in the 1990s the interest had shifted towards those exchange rate regimes which could potentially decrease probability of currency crisis. The view has emerged that in a world of high capital mobility, not only soft exchange rate pegs but also hard pegs may represent invitation to speculative attacks and thus only extreme choices – free float, currency board, and dollarization – are viable. Meanwhile, it has become clear that even currency boards are not immune to speculative attacks. This increased the interest in full dollarization.

The main attraction of official dollarization is the elimination of the risk of sharp exchange rate changes. Official dollarization can also lead to lower spreads on international borrowing, decreasing fiscal costs for both the government and the private sector. Naturally with dollarization sovereign risk remains since government default remains. This still may represent the source of relatively high interest rates. One can think about an example in which dollarized country borrows on higher interest rates than non-dollarized country having flexible exchange rate arrangement since in the latter the currency and the default risk together are lower than the default risk in the former country.

Monetary Union

In a monetary union a set of countries introduces a common currency issued by a common, regional central bank. "Monetary policy is determined at the regional level; seignorage accrues to the region. No option to adjust par-values internally; externally, the monetary authority issuing the common currency can pursue any exchange rate policy." Ghosh, Gulde and Wolf (2002, p.40).

The monetary union has permanently fixed exchange rates within the union and a single central bank sets the interest rate for the union. In such arrangements sovereign country gives up its domestic currency and uses common currency as a legal tender.

VANISHING INTERMEDIATE EXCHANGE RATE REGIMES?

During the 1990s currency crisis hit countries in which pegged exchange rate arrangements prevailed. This happened during the 1992-1993 in the European Exchange Rate Mechanism, in 1994-95 Mexico, in 1997 in South-East Asia, in May 1997 in the Czech Republic, in 1998 in Russia, in 1999 in Ecuador, in 1999 in Brazil, in 2001 in Turkey, and in early 2002 in Argentina. Calvo and Mishkin (2003) call these arrangements 'soft pegs,' indicating that such arrangements were not sufficient to protect the currency. Practically, these regimes were either hard pegs or pegged but adjustable regimes or target zones with relatively tight bands, as a peg with 2.25% band in the European Exchange Rate Mechanism. In most cases currency had been stable for long enough to support the belief that it would continue to stay stable also in the future.

Consequently, an active discussion evolved – which began already after the 1992 events in Europe - on how exchange rate arrangements might have contributed to these crises. Some, most notably Eichengreen (1994), argued that to prevent future crisis either much increased flexibility or true rigidity is needed, implying that both might have ability to prevent speculative attacks. This hypothesis began to be called hypothesis of the vanishing intermediate exchange rate regime, or 'bipolar view' or 'corner solutions' to the exchange rate arrangements. Frankel, Fajnzylber, Schmukler and Serven (2001) define this proposition as 'emerging market countries are, or should be, abandoning basket pegs, crawling pegs, bands, adjustable pegs, and various combinations of these." (p. 352).

The hypothesis of the vanishing intermediate exchange rate regime appears to be a corollary of the impossible trinity hypothesis stating that a country must give up one of three goals: exchange rate stability, monetary independence and financial market integration. Eichengreen (1994) makes an argument that in the future it will not be viable to adopt such policy rules, which intend to achieve an explicitly stated exchange rate level. The implication is that countries that have traditionally pegged their currencies will be forced to choose between fully flexible and very rigid exchange rate arrangements. Eichengreen writes that Kenen had already argued that growing international capital mobility will rule out the maintenance of pegged but adjustable rates, forcing countries to choose between hard pegs and floating currencies. In arguing that fixed rates between currencies are no longer viable and that the choice is between float and monetary unification, Eichengreen takes Kenen's argument forward.

Frankel (1999) agrees that if financial markets are becoming integrated, then the choice is between the exchange rate stability and monetary independence. However, he argues that there is nothing to prevent a country from pursuing a managed float in which half of every fluctuation in demand for its currency is accommodated by intervention and half is allowed to be reflected in the exchange rate. The only recommendation one can give to most central bankers in vulnerable countries is to stay on their toes, Frankel (1999) advises. Furthermore, recommendation to avoid intermediate regimes would not be appropriate says Frankel (1999).

Cooper (1999) takes the argument further by stating that floating rates, independent monetary policy, and freedom of capital movements may also be incompatible, at least for countries with small and poorly developed domestic capital markets. He argues that price levels of small open economies are strongly influenced by exchange rates, and when the exchange rate is not anchored, and when the central bank does not have sufficient reserves it is increasingly difficult to resist movements of market driven by large shocks. For example, a large financial player can influence the exchange rate, hence the price level by selling currency short, and given the dynamics of thin financial markets, a single player can start a run on the currency. Later many may join and depreciation is difficult to avoid. The unwelcome conclusion that flows from Cooper (1999) is that free movements of capital and floating exchange rates are basically incompatible, except for large and diversified economies with well-developed financial markets. Cooper (1999) concludes that unless countries are prepared to fix permanently their currencies to strong currency, or to adopt strong currency as their national money, they may choose to preserve capital controls.

Frankel, Fajnzylber, Schmukler and Serven (2001) write that the vanishing intermediate regime proposition has become fashionable without analytical rationale. They provide analytical rationale for the proposition by introducing the notion of verifiability. They argue that a simple regime (rigid or flexible) may be more verifiable by market participants than a complicated intermediate exchange rate regime and by this fact the simple regime can decrease the uncertainty in the exchange rate markets. "If we are right that it is hard for a central bank to establish credibility for its proclaimed monetary regime without verifiability, then our results confirm that complicated combinations of baskets, crawls, and bands are less likely to satisfy skeptical investors than are simpler regimes." (Frankel, Fajnzylber, Schmukler and Serven, 2001, p. 384).

Calvo and Mishkin (2003) note that the discussion about vanishing intermediate exchange rate regimes is to a certain extent misleading since we have empirical examples, which show that under certain condition neither of the bipolar options work. Collapse of Argentina at the beginning of this century is one example. Argentina was on the currency board with high reserves to back the base and in addition it secured different channels to support the currency in case of unexpected events, and still - due mostly to irresponsible domestic policy – rigid currency arrangement has collapsed. Velde and Veracierto (2000) show that in Argentina different ways to provide additional liquidity were guaranteed. For example, the reserve requirements were changed and banks were to meet the requirements with a variety of interest bearing dollar-denominated financial instruments held with a put option against an A-rate foreign bank. Furthermore Central Bank accumulated reserves in excess of the requirements of the convertibility law. In addition deposit insurance fund was created to which banks were to contribute based on a risk-adjusted basis. Furthermore

Argentina arranged a collection of contingent repurchase contracts with a consortium of private foreign banks; each contract gave the central bank the right to enter at any time of its choosing, and for duration between 2-5 years into a repurchase agreement of Argentine government bonds for U.S. dollars. There were significant costs associated with these facilities, but at times it seemed that there were sufficient funds. Put together Argentina got protection for almost 40% of its deposits or more than 2.5 times the level of the monetary base. This was an extensive protection even in comparison with a central bank with the discretionary power to act as a lender of last resort; Velde and Veracierto (2000).

On the other hand, fully flexible exchange rate regimes are as well not protected against currency crisis. The argument of 'fear of floating' – introduced by Calvo and Reinhart (2002) – holds, i.e. we observe certain reluctance of monetary authorities to allow free fluctuations in their currency. In other words even if the monetary authorities prefer float they also need to avoid depreciation of domestic currency which could hurt the domestic financial system.

Bubula and Otker-Robe (2002) provide some empirical evidence, which helps to evaluate the validity of the vanishing intermediate exchange rate proposition. They provide data about percentage representations of different exchange rate regimes across countries. Bubula and Otker-Robe (2002, p. 16) classify all exchange rate arrangements into hard pegs (dollarization, currency unions and currency boards), intermediate regimes (conventional fixed peg arrangements, crawling pegs, target zones, tightly managed floats) and floating regime (managed floats with no pre-determined path for the currency, and free float). Comparing 1990 to 2001 Bubula and Otker-Robe (2002) show that both hard pegs and floating regimes importance has increased. In 1990 hard pegs represented 15.7% of exchange rate arrangements across the world, while in 2001 this has increased to 25.8%. The increase for floating arrangements was even higher from 15.1% in 1990 to 35.5% in 2001. Combined, the 'corner solutions' represented 30.9% in 1990 as compared to 61.% in 2001. This gives a certain support for the view that intermediate regimes importance is decreasing across the globe, however still in 2001 intermediate regimes represented almost 40% of exchange rate arrangements. While we observe a movement towards corner solutions worldwide, this tendency is the most pronounced among the developed and emerging market countries and less among the developing countries. As Bubula and Otker-Robe (2002) show in developed countries in 2001 hard pegs represented 54.2% of all arrangements, and floats 41.7%. Similarly in emerging markets the hard pegs represented 32.1% and floats 46.4% in 2001. Thus, the intermediate regimes represented only 4.2% for developed world and 21.4% for emerging markets in 2001. Among developing countries we observe a decline in the spread of intermediate regimes, from 68.4% in 1990 to 43.8% in 2001, but still intermediate regimes represent almost a half of all arrangements.

Calvo and Mishkin (2003) also point to the fact that certain institutional features of emerging markets may make the decision about optimal exchange rate regime more difficult than is in the case of developed countries. Among these they refer to vulnerable fiscal, financial, and monetary institution; currency substitution, liability dollarization, and increased vulnerability to sudden stops of capital inflows. The worst scenario begins with irresponsible fiscal policy, which forces the central bank to monetize the debt which ultimately weakens domestic currency. "A floating exchange rate is clearly the wrong prescription for this situation, since it allows the sharp depreciation that cripples balance sheets and the financial sector. But under the dual stresses of weak institutions and sudden stops, it is not clear that a fixed exchange rate is sustainable either." Calvo and Mishkin (2003, p. 13). Thus, it seems that it is the proper economic policy or improvement in fiscal, financial, and monetary institutions which these countries need to concentrate in order to avoid possibility of currency crisis.

De Jure and De Facto Exchange Rate Arrangements

After the breakdown of the Bretton Woods system a wide variety of exchange rate regimes emerged across the world. This was supported by the new Article IV of the Amendment to the Articles of Agreement of the IMF, which confirmed the member country's freedom to choose its exchange rate regime. To get a picture about the share of different exchange rate regimes one considers domestic government official proclamation about the exchange rate regime of the country. This official statement is based on the self-declaration of the domestic governments and as such is reported to the International Monetary Fund. This is published by the International Monetary Fund in its Annual Report on Exchange Rate Arrangements and Exchange Restrictions. Countries are to inform the IMF within 30 days of becoming a member about their exchange rate arrangements and they are to inform the IMF if this arrangement is changed. This official record at IMF captures the formal commitment of domestic government to an exchange rate regime. For example in Spring 1999 out of 185 member countries the IMF classifies 47 as having float, 45 rigid pegs and 93 intermediate regime. Fischer (2001)

IMF exchange rate regime classification has evolved from 1950 till early period of this century. For example during the Bretton Woods period, between 1950 and 1973, IMF classification recognized two options: par value and other than par value. The first option was the fixed but adjustable peg option and the second dealt with countries which for different reasons for a shorter or longer time period did not participate in the Bretton Woods arrangements.

In the period from 1973 till 1983 IMF classification recognized basically two types of exchange rate regimes. The division line was between exchange rate maintained within relatively narrow margins in terms of strong currencies and arrangements not maintained within relatively narrow margins. In the period 1983 till 1996 IMF introduced four categories of de jure exchange rate arrangements: a peg to a currency (composite of currencies), limited flexibility, a more flexible arrangement, and an independent float.

The exchange rate regime classification introduced by the International Monetary Fund from 1999 recognizes no separate legal tender, currency board, conventional peg with a band of at most ± 1%, peg with horizontal bands larger than ± 1%, crawling peg, crawling band, managed float with no pre-announced path, and independent float as exchange rate regimes; Reinhart and Rogoff (2002), von Hagen and Zhou (2002).

Typically, the IMF has taken as given the domestic country's exchange rate declaration. In other words the IMF did not check whether there was a difference between the de facto and the de jure exchange rate regime.

There is a variety of reasons which may lead to difference between de jure and de facto regimes. For example it happens that the pre-announced de jure band is much wider than the de facto band in which the currency moves. More stable behavior of the exchange rate may be a result of intentional policy action, but currency may be more stable also because there are no shocks to move it away from stable path. Also, it may happen that country declares flexible exchange rate regime but in reality it heavily intervenes so that the currency behaves as if fixed exchange rate regime was in use. On the other hand, country might claim pegged regime, however having frequent devaluations could make this regime less distinct from a more flexible one.

These differences led researchers to search for algorithms, which may establish the discrepancy between de jure and de facto regimes. While systematic treatment of this issue is relatively new, the difference between de jure and de facto regimes was observed long ago. "It is well known that some countries with ostensibly floating exchange rates intervene regularly in the foreign exchange market to stabilize the rate, whereas others with pegged exchange rates avail themselves of such wide intervention margins that the currency's value is determined within very wide limits by market forces." Heller (1978, p.308).

Some studies attempted to extend the official classification into a more meaningful one, as for example Ghosh, Gulde, Ostry and Wolf (1997), Bubula and Otker-Robe (2002), and Reinhard and Rogoff (2003). Some others rely on purely statistical methods in order to re-classify exchange rate regimes as Levy-Yeyati and Sturzenegger (2003). Bubula and Otker-Robe (2002) construct a database for all IMF member countries for the period 1990 – 2001. Reinhard and Rogoff (2003) present a classification based on monthly database for 153 countries over the period 1946-2001.

Levy-Yeyati and Sturzenegger (2003) use an algorithm, which takes into consideration changes and volatility of changes of the exchange rate and also volatility of international reserves. They use textbook argumentation that fixed exchange rates are associated with changes in international reserves to reduce exchange rate volatility, and floats are characterized by volatility in rates with relatively stable reserves. Levy-Yeyati and Sturzenegger (2003, p. 2).

Levy-Yeyati and Sturzenegger (2003) capture exchange rate policies on the basis of actual behavior of three variables. These are exchange rate volatility, volatility of exchange rate changes and volatility of reserves. They classify the exchange rate de facto arrangements into four groups. Flexible exchange rate regime is defined as having high exchange rate volatility as well as high volatility of exchange rate changes, but low volatility of international reserves. Fixed regime is defined with low volatility of exchange rate as well as low volatility of exchange rate changes, but high volatility of international reserves. In addition, they define dirty float, which in difference to flexible regime has also high volatility of reserves and crawling peg, which in difference to fixed regime has high exchange rate volatility. They observe in empirical data what they call 'inconclusive' regimes where all these variables take the 'low' value. However, – as Bubula and Otker-Robe (2002, p.9) mention – Levy-Yeyati and Sturzenegger's classification may lead to cases in which country is considered as an inconclusive case when in its exchange rate regime is simply obvious. Bubula and Otker-Robe also question the reliance of Levy-Yeyati and Sturzenegger on the cluster analysis. "The regime classification generated by this approach are not robust to the choice of the number of countries in the sample and the number of clusters specified ex-ante by the user." Bubula and Otker-Robe (2002, p.9)

Bubula and Otker-Robe (2002) introduce an exchange rate regime classification, which takes into the consideration the combination of the de jure and de facto characteristics of the exchange rate regimes. Their classification is a step forward as compared to Levy-Yeyati and Sturzenegger (2003) since Levy-Yeyati and Sturzenegger ignore the official classification on the whole. Bubula and Otker-Robe (2002) use a combination of quantitative and qualitative analysis, i.e. they do not depend solely on the quantitative analysis but also use adjustments based on consultation with member countries and IMF country desk economists. Bubula and Otker-Robe (2002, p.15). They classify into the hard peg category dollarization, currency union and currency board, while to the floating regime they include independent floats and managed float with no pre-determined path for the currency. The remaining categories belong to inter-mediate arrangements in their classification.

Reinhart and Rogoff (2003) provide classification of exchange rate regimes, which takes into consideration the existence of black or parallel exchange rate markets. They distinguish fourteen categories of exchange rate regimes. These are no separate legal tender, pre-announced peg or currency board arrangement, pre–announced horizontal band that is narrower than or equal to ± 2%, de facto peg, pre-announced crawling peg, pre-announced crawling band that is narrower than or equal to ±2%, de facto crawling peg, de facto crawling band that is narrower than or equal to ± 2%, pre-announced crawling band that is wider than or equal to ± 2%, de facto crawling band that is narrower than or equal to ±5 %, moving band that is narrower than or equal to ± 2% (i.e. allows for both appreciation and depreciation over time), managed floating, freely floating, and freely falling exchange rate regime. Introduction of freely falling exchange rate regime reflects a deep insight known in discussions in exchange rate economics but not incorporated so far into the classification or exchange rate regimes. It is known already from the Nurkse – Friedman debate that one should avoid a fallacy when associating float with periods of great turmoil and as a result suggest that floating rates were responsible for the turmoil. As McCallum (1996) writes it is possible that periods of extraordinary instability are those in which the shocks happen to be very large. These large shocks are then likely to set off turbulence under which it is difficult to keep exchange rates stable.

Reinhart and Rogoff (2003, p. 26) find that "across all countries for 1970-2001, 45 percent of the observations officially labeled as a 'peg' should, in fact, have been classified as limited flexibility, managed or freely floating – or worse, 'freely falling." The pair-wise correlation coefficient between their exchange rate regime classification and the official IMF classification is 0.42. Furthermore, for the Post-Bretton-Woods period they find that exchange rate regimes labeled as managed floats were more than in half of the cases de facto pegs or crawling pegs.

Hausmann, Panizza and Stein (2001) investigated behavior of those 38 developed and developing countries which de jure have adopted floating exchange rate regimes or target zones with very wide band. They show that "these countries have very different level of international reserves, and allow very different degrees of flexibility of the exchange rate relative to the volatility of their reserves or of the interest rate." (p. 412). There was a marked difference between the behavior of the G-3 countries which float with a very low level of reserves and allow a high volatility of their currency relative to reserves and interest rates, while the almost opposite holds for the emerging market countries. Hausmann, Panizza and Stein (2001) find a robust relationship between the ability to borrow internationally in own currency and the behavior of exchange rate under de jure floating regime. They conclude that "floating rate countries that do not borrow internationally in their own currency tend to hold significantly larger reserve levels, and to allow much less volatility in the exchange rate relative to their interventions." (p. 413). They measure the ability to borrow internationally in own currency as the ratio between the stock of international debt securities issued by a country in its own currency and the total stock of securities issued by the country in all currencies.

Von Hagen and Zhou (2002) rightly point to the fact that the difference between de jure and de facto exchange rate regimes does not mean that the de jure classification is irrelevant since official regimes are likely to guide financial market expectations and thus affect policy decisions.

Chapter 2

How to Choose an Exchange Rate Regime?

Approaches to Choosing Exchange Rate Regime

The literature on exchange rate regimes distinguishes different approaches to the question of how to choose a proper exchange rate regime.

The first approach takes a macroeconomic model and then evaluates which exchange rate regime could ease the response of the economy to different disturbances. Following Poole (1970), this literature includes among others Fischer (1977), Flood (1979), Frenkel and Aizenman (1982). For a survey see Argy (1990). In summary a country exposed to external nominal shocks should use flexible rates to insulate the domestic economy. On the other hand, a fixed regime can be useful when dealing with domestic nominal shocks, while domestic real shocks are best handled under a flexible regime. Domestic money demand and money supply shocks, i.e. domestic nominal shocks, can potentially lead to inflation and currency depreciation and fixed exchange rate can accommodate these changes with less output volatility. On the other hand, real shocks, as shocks to productivity, can be best accommodated – in terms of output stability - under flexible regimes. This approach has relatively little practical application since most of the economies face various combinations of real, nominal, domestic and external shocks. It seems that it is not practical to select an exchange rate regime based on this approach, even if the results have conceptual validity.

The second approach deals with the problem of the exchange rate regime in the context of stabilization plans; see for example Dornbusch (1986), Dornbusch et al. (1990), Bruno (1991), and Blanchard et al. (1991). It considers a country with high inflation that wishes to stabilize while minimizing the costs of adjustment. The stabilizing country first needs to correct the source of its imbalances (usually some deficit). However, correction of fundamentals would usually not suffice. Bruno (1991) shows that the corrected system can be consistent with different inflation rates. For this reason a clear signal of a shift in policy is needed, which is usually provided by a firm nominal anchor.

The third approach is based on the credibility versus flexibility trade-off and is built on the work of Barro and Gordon (1983) and generally on the time inconsistency literature. This approach represented typically by the work of Giavazzi and Giovannini (1989) and Fratianni and von Hagen (1992) puts forward the idea that exchange rate peg can help in importing credibility for domestic economy. This means that country with (relatively) high inflation experience and thus lower credibility of its monetary authorities could import credibility from a country which in time has already proved its firm commitment to low inflation and stable currency.

The fourth approach is empirical and combines features of other approaches. Heller (1978) and Melvin (1985) are early attempts in this approach while Edwards (1996), Berger, Sturm and de Haan (2000) and von Hagen and Zhou (2002) are more recent contributions. Heller (1978) using discriminant analysis takes the de jure classification of the exchange rate regimes by the IMF as given and establishes macro-economic characteristics of countries choosing a particular exchange rate regime. His results indicate that those countries, which float are of large size with small foreign trade sector, with high degree of international financial integration, with inflation behavior different from the world average and have diversified foreign trade pattern. The opposite characteristics are of pegging countries. Von Hagen and Zhou (2002) distinguish three groups of factors affecting a country's exchange rate regime choice: economic fundamentals, variables relating to macroeconomic stabilization and variables relating to the risk of currency crisis.

The fifth approach is rooted in the theory of optimal currency areas. This approach investigates the structural characteristics that determine whether maintaining internal and external balance is better achieved with fixed or floating rates. We review this approach later in this chapter.

The sixth approach would consider ex post macroeconomic performance under different exchange rate arrangements. It would be a natural choice to decide on proper exchange rate arrangement based on past macroeconomic performance connected with different types of these arrangements. We shortly review this approach later in the chapter.

In the remaining part of this Chapter we present the basic modeling background for understanding the credibility-flexibility trade-off in choosing the exchange rate regime. We also discuss the basic modeling approach to the issue of exchange rate regime and currency crisis. Furthermore, we provide a review of the optimum currency area literature, and we close with short review of the literature on macroeconomic performance and exchange rate arrangements.

Credibility – Flexibility Trade-Off

Policy-makers have an objective function, which gives a positive weight to stimulation of employment and a negative weight to inflation, and if in addition the real wage is above the market-clearing rate, the demand for labor becomes the binding constraint on employment. Thus, an un-anticipated inflation can reduce the real wage and temporarily increase employment.

A very useful framework in which one can think about such situations is the time inconsistency framework in which in equilibrium positive inflation is produced as a result of the game between government and the labor. Ultimately, policy makers do not succeed in pushing employment above its natural level but the attempt leads to an equilibrium positive inflation. A lower rate of inflation could have been achieved if prior to signing of nominal contracts government would have credibly committed itself to lower rate of inflation. So when government has the discretion to pick inflation after the settlements of contracts, a positive inflation may arise. This basic setting is typically developed in the time inconsistency framework developed by Barro-Gordon (1983). We follow Walsh (1998).

Assume that the government's loss function is given by quadratic function V.

$$V = \frac{1}{2}\lambda(y - y_n - k)^2 + \frac{1}{2}\pi^2$$

where y is output, y_n is natural rate of output, and π is the inflation rate. Government policy is to minimize the expected value of the loss function V. The parameter λ gives the relative weight that the government places on output expansion relative to inflation stabilization. The central bank desires to stabilize inflation around zero, and output around $[y_n + k]$, which is the second best solution the first would be to eliminate the distortions which lead the existence of k.

Economy is described by a Lucas-type supply function.

$$y = y_n + a(\pi - \pi^e) + e$$

where e is the supply shock, and the parameter α gives the weight to the un-expected inflationary surprise. If actual inflation exceeds the expected rate, real wages decline and firms expand employment, and thus output may grow.

The link between inflation and the central bank's policy instrument is:

$$\pi = \Delta m + v$$

where Δm is the growth rate of the money supply and v is a velocity disturbance. The equilibrium when the central bank acts with discretion produces a positive average rate of inflation. This has no effect on output, since the private sector completely anticipates inflation at this rate. Solution under the quadratic loss function is

$$\Delta m = \frac{a^2\lambda\pi^e - a\lambda e + a\lambda k}{1 + a^2\lambda}$$

Private agents use the information when forming their expectations about inflation and as a result the expected inflation $\pi^e = \lambda a k$. The equilibrium rate of inflation under discretion is positive and is given by:

$$\pi^d = \lambda a k + \frac{-a\lambda}{1 + \lambda a^2} e + v$$

Suppose that the central bank would be able to pre-commit to a policy rule prior to the formation of private expectations. Under a commitment policy, the central bank commits itself to particular values of parameter prior to the public forming its expectations of inflation and prior to observing the particular realization of the shock e. In the simplest case it would lead to

$$\Delta m^{c} = -\frac{a\lambda}{1+a^{2}\lambda}e$$

The average inflation under pre-commitment will be zero but the response to the aggregate supply shock is the same as under discretion. Thus pre-commitment led to better solution than discretion. As Kenen (1994, p. 157) writes this concept represent a pessimistic view of the government which either deliberately misleads agents or is myopic and not able to resist short-run temptation.

One can model the choice of exchange rate regime in the above framework, too. For example Berger, Jensen and Schjelderup (2001) model the credibility – flexibility trade-off in the above framework with incorporating exchange rates.

$$y = \alpha(\pi - \pi^{e}) + \varepsilon$$

describes the output as the function of actual and expected inflation and a supply shock. Timing is as in the above framework, i.e. first the labor settles wage contracts, then supply shock is observed and thereafter the authorities perform monetary policy. We assume in difference to the above, that inflation is controlled directly, and that purchasing power parity holds.

$$\pi = e + \pi^{*} + \phi$$

where π^{*} is the foreign inflation rate, e is the nominal exchange rate and ϕ is the shock. The monetary policy is to minimize deviations of inflation and output from their target levels.

To choose between the flexible and fixed exchange rate regime one would need to obtain the equilibrium values for inflation and output, and then based on these results compare the loss function under the flexible and fixed exchange rate regime. The time consistent equilibrium values were:

$$\pi = \lambda\alpha y^{*} - \frac{\lambda\alpha}{1+\lambda\alpha^{2}}\varepsilon$$

This contains the inflation bias since there is the incentive for expansive monetary policy to raise the output.

$$y = \frac{1}{1+\lambda\alpha^{2}}\varepsilon$$

Under flexible regimes the value of the foreign inflation and foreign shock ϕ does not enter the equilibrium values since the movement in these variables is compensated by the movement in the exchange rate, *e*.

Loss function under floating rates will equal to

$$L^{flex} = \lambda y^{*2} + \lambda^2 \alpha^2 y^{*2} + \frac{\lambda}{(1+\lambda\alpha^2)^2}\sigma_\varepsilon^2 + \frac{\lambda^2\alpha^2}{(1+\lambda\alpha^2)^2}\sigma_\varepsilon^2$$

where σ_ε^2 is the variance of the supply shock.

In difference the loss function of monetary authorities under the fixed exchange rate regime equals to

$$L^{fix} = \lambda y^{*2} + \pi^{*2} + \lambda[\sigma_\varepsilon^2 + \alpha^2\sigma_\phi^2 + 2\alpha\rho\sigma_\varepsilon\sigma_\phi] + \sigma_\phi^2$$

where ρ describes the correlation coefficient between the two shocks.

Berger, Jensen and Schjelderup (2001) show that when deciding which exchange rate regime to choose the authorities choose the fixed regime if $L^{fix} < L^{flex}$ which in this model equals to:

$$\lambda^2\alpha^2 y^{*2} - \pi^{*2} > \lambda[\sigma_\varepsilon^2 + \alpha^2\sigma_\phi^2 + 2\alpha\rho\sigma_\varepsilon\sigma_\phi] - \frac{\lambda}{(1+\lambda\alpha^2)^2}\sigma_\varepsilon^2 + \sigma_\phi^2 - \frac{\lambda^2\alpha^2}{(1+\lambda\alpha^2)^2}\sigma_\varepsilon^2$$

This inequality states that the peg is beneficial if the credibility gain is larger than the loss of flexibility. That can be seen more easily if we for example assume that the ϕ shocks are zero. Then the above expression simplifies to

$$\lambda^2\alpha^2 y^{*2} - \pi^{*2} > \frac{\lambda^2\alpha^2}{1+\lambda\alpha^2}\sigma_\varepsilon^2$$

The left-hand side expression needs to be positive for the introduction of fixed exchange rate regime to make sense, since this is the difference between (squared) equilibrium average inflation under flexible and fixed regimes. In other words it exhibits the regime difference in terms of losses from average inflation, while the right hand side represents weighted regime difference in terms of losses from output variance; Berger, Jensen and Schjelderup (2001, p.3).

Currency Crisis Considerations

In the 1990s world has witnessed currency crisis almost on all continents. In September 1992 British pound dropped out from the Exchange Rate Mechanism (ERM), followed by the

Italian lira, Spanish peseta was devalued; in 1993 as a result of speculative attacks bands were widened in the ERM. In December 1994 Mexico witnessed currency crisis, in May 1997 the Czech Republic, then in summer 1997 Asian currency crisis hit a large number of countries. Then Russia, Brazil, Turkey and Argentina followed. Most of these crises were to a certain extent consequence of improper exchange rate arrangements, which reflected deeper structural problems in these economies as well as their increased exposure to liberalized financial markets.

Most of the recent currency crisis occurred under pegged regimes. Currency crisis occurs if the speculative attack causes the exchange rate to depreciate or forces the authorities to defend it by radically raising interest rates or expending reserves. Currency crisis may occur also if there is an attack to strengthen the domestic currency and get it out of the band and thus weaken government policy commitment.

In this section we present the two basic types of models which provide certain explanation and rationale for currency crisis. We begin with the first generation models, which are also called Fed type classical models and are based on insights of Salant and Henderson (1978) that the fixed price of gold backed by a government-held stock should end in a speculative attack eliminating that stock. The two classical papers in this field are Krugman (1979) and Flood and Garber (1984). In these papers governments are assumed to have a need to monetize budget deficits and then face crisis when domestic and international commitments collide.

Second generation models have circular arguments built into them so that speculation against a currency creates conditions that increase the probability of devaluation. Thus, pegged rates that could be sustained in the absence of an attack are susceptible to attack and thus susceptible to collapse. It is not that in these models economic fundamentals are not important, but there exist a zone in which multiple solutions are possible and which solution prevails will depend on the psychology of the market and on the strength of the speculators.

We present the Flood-Garber model, which is the workhorse of the first generation modeling approach. In the exposure of the model we follow Flood and Garber (1984) and Obstfeld and Rogoff (1996). In this model government consists of two branches. A fiscal authority runs an exogenously determined deficit and the monetary authority is required to monetize this deficit. Monetary authority has an external obligation to keep the exchange rate regime and an internal obligation to monetize the government deficit. This inconsistency implies that the peg must give way to a flexible exchange rate arrangement.

This is a monetary model of a small economy presented in continuous time, with perfect foresight. The small country assumption means that the foreign price level as well as the foreign interest rate will be considered as exogenous.

Model uses five equations:

$$\frac{M_t}{P_t} = \alpha_0 - \alpha_1 i_t \qquad \alpha_1 > 0$$

This equation represents the money demand function, which relates the demand for real money balances negatively to nominal interest rates. Notation is the following: t is the time index, M_t denotes nominal money balances, P_t domestic price level, i_t domestic nominal interest rate, and a_0 and a_1 are parameters.

$$M_t = R_t + D_t$$

This equation defines money supply as the sum of the domestic credit, D_t, and the foreign exchange reserves, R_t.

$$\dot{D}_t = \mu$$

This equation determines the rate of credit expansion in the economy. Dot over a variable indicates the time derivative.

$$P_t = P_t^* S_t$$

This denotes the purchasing power parity, i.e. that the price of domestic good equals the price of foreign good converted into domestic currency by exchange rate. The foreign price level, P_t* is assumed given, S_t denotes the nominal exchange rate (the domestic price of foreign exchange).

$$i_t = i_t^* + \frac{\dot{S}_t}{S_t}$$

This depicts the interest rate parity, which requires the equality between the domestic interest rate and the foreign interest rate, i_t* adjusted for the rate of depreciation, with foreign interest rate fixed.

In this setting the fixed regime collapses even without a speculative attack, which is seen by finding a reduced form for the exchange rate S_t.

$$M_t = \beta S_t - \alpha \dot{S}_t$$

where α and β are linear combinations of parameters and foreign variables.

If the exchange rate is fixed, then $S_t = \overline{S}$, and $\dot{S}_t = 0$. Then,

$$R_t = \beta \overline{S} - D_t$$

$$\dot{R}_t = -\dot{D}_t = -\mu$$

These equations bring the crucial implication of the model: under a fixed exchange rate regime, the excessive rate of domestic credit is reflected in a depletion of foreign reserves. How fast this depletion occurs depends on the rate of growth of *D*. Model has perfect foresight, and when market participants realize when the regime is unsustainable agents would not wait until the regime collapses, because it would mean a capital loss for them. Thus they will sell the domestic currency before the lower bound is reached. This selling then forces the pegged regime to collapse at earlier time.

A significant contribution of this modeling strategy was that it was possible to determine when currency crisis is going to occur, and thus to show that such crisis could be a result of rational strategies and not only of panics and manias. In this perfect foresight model it is also possible to calculate the time of the collapse, which will be function of reserves at the beginning period (large amount of reserves potentially delays the collapse) and of the domestic credit growth.

Currency crisis models of the second generation are based on an idea that there are number of channels through which a speculative attack could undermine the peg that would otherwise have been sustainable. Obstfeld (1994) develops a model in Barro-Gordon framework in which incompatible policy goals combined with private agents' expectations destroy a pegged exchange rate arrangement, when the fundamentals are sound. These models create circularity leading to multiple equilibria.

In this model the domestic output is given by:

$$y_t = \alpha(e_t - w_t) - u_t$$

where w_t is the money wage, and u_t is a stochastic disturbance. Output, y_t is given by quasi-labor demand schedule varying inversely with the real wage (w_t-p_t). Workers and firms agree to set period t wages w_t on date t-1 so as to maintain constant real wage.

$$w_t = E_{t-1}(e_t)$$

Assume any exchange rate policy holds. The policy maker seeks to minimize costs arising from two sources. First, the loss function will penalize deviations of inflation rate from a target of zero. Since purchasing power parity holds, and foreign price level equals zero, then the domestic inflation is $e_t - e_{t-1}$. Second, it also penalizes deviations of output from a target y^*. The target output y^* is positive. The government loss for period t is:

$$L_t = \frac{\theta}{2}(e_t - e_{t-1})^2 + \frac{1}{2}[\alpha(e_t - w_t) - u_t - y^*]^2$$

The problem may be that government cannot commit to pre-announced future actions. So the government problem would be to minimize the loss function subject to previous equations. Then

$$e_t - e_{t-1} = \lambda w_t + \frac{\lambda}{\alpha}u_t + \frac{\lambda}{\alpha}y^* - \lambda e_{t-1}$$

where λ is a parameter. This condition says that government uses the exchange rate partially to offset shocks u_t to output. Since wages were set one period ahead, the government may find it optimal to use 'surprise' depreciation, whenever wage inflation risk erodes competitiveness. Workers and firms set the wages accordingly.

$$w_t = e_{t-1} + \frac{\lambda}{(1-\lambda)\alpha} y^*$$

Which leads to equilibrium depreciation rate:

$$e_t - e_{t-1} = \frac{\lambda}{(1-\lambda)\alpha} y^* + \frac{\lambda}{\alpha} u_t$$

Notice that unless lambda is zero, the economy is afflicted by systematic inflation. A fixed exchange rate would eliminate this inflation bias, but it would also prevent the government from responding to unpredictable output shocks.

Furthermore, Obstfeld (1994) assumes that a new type of costs appears in loss function. Note Z=1 if there is a change in exchange rate, Z=0 otherwise. Loss function then changes into the following.

$$L_t = \frac{\theta}{2}(e_t - e_{t-1})^2 + \frac{1}{2}[\alpha(e_t - w_t) - u_t - y^*]^2 + cZ$$

If the government realigns then it incurs the fixed costs *c*, and its loss is:

$$L_t^R = \frac{1}{2}(1-\lambda)[\alpha\pi + u_t + y^*]^2 + c$$

Realignment occurs when the difference in the loss function between keeping the peg and realigning would be positive, i.e. $L_t^{fix} - L_t^{realign} > 0$, which equals to

$$\frac{1}{2}\lambda[\alpha\pi_t + u_t + y^*]^2 > c$$

The inequality above is the realignment rule, sometimes also called an escape-clause arrangement; if it holds then re-alignment occurs. The realignment costs, *c*, are imposed to ensure that during normal times the authorities have the incentive to maintain the peg. In principle such an escape clause arrangement may raise welfare, since it allows exchange rate flexibility when it is most needed, and it restrains the inflationary pressures otherwise.

However, in the practice to implement such clauses is difficult since π (expected inflation) is in the game also. Thus, expectations of inflation (depreciation) depend on market perceptions whether the realignment occurs or not. This element introduces circularity and the potential for multiple equilibria.

Optimum Currency Areas Considerations

This section is based on the working paper published in the Bank of Finland, Bofit Discussion Paper Series, 2003/15.

Optimal currency area (OCA) theory deals with complicated, inter-mingled issues at the core of international macroeconomics. OCA theory's main applications are found, to my best knowledge, in three areas.

First, OCA theory has reshaped the discussion on selection of an exchange rate regime for a given country. Although the criteria developed under OCA theory are not easily put into practice, the substantial literature on selecting exchange rate regimes well documents the rise to prominence of OCA theory in the analysis used in selection of an exchange rate regime. Second, OCA theory provides considerable insight into the role of exchange rate adjustment under balance of payment disequilibria. The extensive empirical literature on measuring the symmetry and asymmetry of shocks to countries and regions well documents this impact. Third, OCA theory has contributed to the theory of monetary integration and has been fundamental in the design of Europe's Economic and Monetary Union (EMU). It also provides a standard point of departure in discussions of dollarization and creation of new monetary unions. This view concurs with Bofinger (1994), who, despite his criticism of the theory, writes that OCA theory "seems to be almost generally accepted as the main touchstone of the advantages of EMU and as the theoretical basis for all empirical tests in this area."

Broadly speaking, optimum currency area theory deals with relationships among countries, regions, and currencies. The world is not a unity in a political sense; it is divided into almost two hundred independent countries, most are further divided into distinct regions. Currency considerations may take a fairly low priority at the time a new state is formed. For example, the dozens of new countries that emerged after the collapse of colonial empires, as well as those created after the collapse of the Soviet empire, all belong to currency areas. Yet, despite this foreseeable economic consequence of independence, there is surprisingly little discussion of optimal currency area issues preceding the disintegration of former colonial or socialist countries. Willett (2001, p. 3) writes, "It is true that common currency areas are sometimes split apart as nations split apart, as has occurred recently with Czechoslovakia and Yugoslavia, but there is little reason to think that OCA considerations played any role in their desolution." As few studies look at the disintegration effects from the currency perspective. See Fidrmuc, Horvath, and Fidrmuc (1999) on the breakup of Czechoslovakia.

On the other hand, optimum currency area criteria have been (and to some extent still are) at the core of the discussion on Western European integration. Questions, for example, as to the degree Western Europe was an optimal currency area, were at the forefront of the integration debate.

For a country like the United States with relatively permanent political borders, the discussion of optimal currency areas might appear moot. In fact, several studies consider whether the US constitutes an optimum currency area. Ghosh and Wolf (1994), for example, conclude the US is not an optimum currency area and tentatively suggest separate currencies for different parts of the United States.

One needs to limit the currency area before considering its optimality. A currency area is an area in which exchange rates are fixed, or which has a common currency. Under the modern concept of "one country, one currency," practically any country can be considered a currency area. A currency area thus corresponds to optimum currency area to the extent as the political considerations for creation of the country correspond to the economic considerations of currency optimality. This brings up the Mundell's great question as to what is the appropriate domain of a currency area: How large should the territory using a single currency be?

The Mundellian question is traditionally framed in two ways. First, is a country, say x, an optimum currency area? Does x possess such characteristics that allow it to use its currency optimally throughout the country or would separate parts (regions) of x be better off with their own regional currencies? Second, there is the supranational perspective. Would x be better off as part of a larger currency area and without a separate currency? Melitz (1995, p. 496). Demopoulos and Yannacopoulos (1999, p. 290) argue these two approaches are not in conflict and each serves its own purpose.

One can also approach the Mundellian problem from another angle. It is commonly accepted that monetary exchange is more advantageous than barter, so if it is advantageous to use monetary exchange (currency) in a small territory, why not to enlarge this territory to gain the advantages of money over barter in a larger space. How far is appropriate in the territorial enlargement of a currency?

The ideal search methodology would consider the world economy and indicate how to divide it into optimum currency areas. Grubel (1970, p. 319) notes that this would require determining the levels of world welfare under different currency arrangements so that the optimum currency area would be an area where this welfare is maximized. Mundell (1961) and the subsequent literature dealt with more tractable problems. The interest moved toward the search for criteria that would "define the optimum currency area, within which the exchange rates should be pegged immutably, but whose rates should fluctuate, or at least be varied, vis-à-vis the outside world." Kenen (1969, p. 41).

Usage of the terms "optimal" and "optimum" in the context of OCA theory varies. McKinnon (1963) writes that optimum applies to a currency area where three objectives are sustained: full employment, a stable price level, and a balanced external account. The first two objectives pertain to internal equilibria, the last to external equilibrium. McKinnon (1963, p. 717). Kenen (1969) offers a similar definition: "If the prevailing exchange-rate regime, fixed or flexible, can maintain external balance without causing unemployment (or, on the other side, demand-induced wage inflation), that regime is optimal." Kenen (1969, p. 41). Kenen (1969) notes that optimality should be judged from both the global viewpoint and the viewpoint of the individual country. Grubel (1970) explains that "optimal" is used in to describe "the union between a number of regions or countries, which improves welfare of the population resident within these territories above the level enjoyed when each was a separate currency area." Grubel (1970, p. 319). Grubel (1970) also considers the welfare of residents in a particular country as a function of the level and stability of the real income and the level of national economic independence. Allen and Kenen (1980) write that "optimal" in OCA theory indicates a minimization of the costs of balance-of-payments adjustment. Allen and Kenen (1980, pp. 381-396). Melitz (1995) argues that it makes sense to speak about optimality when the question is "what the optimum enlargement of the currency area would be from the standpoint of the individual country or region in question." However, he argues that if we take the size of a currency area as given we already cannot speak about optimality, but only about welfare improving. Melitz, (1995, p. 496). Ricci asserts, "The nature of the issue makes it impossible to find a rule of thumb for the identification of an optimum currency area (defined as a currency are in which all members expect positive net benefits from their participation)." Ricci (1997, p. 33). Rather than attempt to classify these definitions, I defer to the early observation of Mundell (1961, p. 717): "The idea of optimality ... is complex and difficult to quantify precisely."

Such non-rigorous theorizing partly explains the disparate views about OCA theory. Ingram observed, "I confess that I do not think the question of an optimum currency area is any longer a very interesting one." Ingram (1969, p. 96). Johnson dismisses the theory as "something of a dead-end problem." Johnson (1973, p. 395). Niehans claims the theory attempts to solve a "prohibitively difficult problem," noting that "the problem is logically similar to the problem of how a country should be divided into voting districts in such a way that the parliamentary seats for a given party are maximized. In its full generality, it is obviously a prohibitively difficult problem, so it is hardly surprising that twenty years of academic efforts have brought little progress toward its solution. What we have is a variety of suggestions about certain elements that may play a role in the solution." Niehans (1984, p. 291). Vaubel argues, "There is no operational scientific method of measuring and comparing the costs and benefits of currency unification for a given group of countries. For the same reasons, as we shall see, there is no operational scientific method of defining optimum currency areas." Vaubel (1990, pp. 174-176). Willett (1994) states that "the theory of optimum currency areas points to many relevant considerations, but not with a level of operational precision that would lead informed economists to always reach the same conclusions." Willett (1994, p. 207). Bofinger (1994, p. 15) writes, "Taking into consideration the obvious flaws of this [OCA] theory, it is surprising that it could experience such wide-spread revival in the early 1990s." Buiter (1995, p. 30) reflects that "the optimal currency area literature is woefully inadequate and confused on the issue what policy institutional or other behavioral changes are necessary in order to compensate for the loss of the nominal exchange rate instrument." Goodhart (1996, p. 1984) simply states, "I do not find this theory [optimum currency area] particularly helpful." Finally, we have the distinctly different view of Krugman (1994): "I would suggest that the issue of optimum currency areas, or, more broadly, that of choosing an exchange rate regime, should be regarded as the central intellectual question of international monetary economics." Tavlas (1993, p. 663).

With more than forty years of the literature on optimum currency areas to consider, I pursue a selective approach. We review the classical contributions, which will involve the groundwork of searching for characteristics (criteria) that could be used to define an OCA. Next, we review some of the modern contributions that reflect developments in international macroeconomics in the last twenty years or so. Finally, we discuss some empirical literature.

Theoretical Contributions to Optimum Currency Area Theory

Mundell (1961) and the Labor Mobility Criterion

In the 1950s, a series of papers questioned Bretton-Woods exchange-rate arrangements under which fixed, but adjustable, exchange rates prevailed. These publications identified adjustment problems under fixed regimes and argued in favor of flexible rates. Mundell (1961) summarizes the argument of proponents of flexible exchange rates: "Depreciation can take the place of unemployment when the external balance is in deficit, and appreciation can replace inflation when it is in surplus." Mundell (1961, p. 657). If flexible exchange rates are more advantageous than fixed rates, Mundell asks, does it follow that all currencies in the world should be flexible? Furthermore, he inquires, are countries the proper units to take advantage of different exchange rate arrangements?

Mundell observes that there would be a major difference "between adjustment within a currency area which has a single currency and a currency area involving more than one currency; in other words there will be a difference between interregional adjustment and international adjustment even though exchange rates, in the latter case, are fixed." ibid. (p. 658). To illustrate this he introduces three examples of adjustment in different areas affected by asymmetric demand shocks. The first example considers two independent countries with national currencies, where each country is also a region. The second considers a country with one currency and two distinct regions. The third involves two countries with independent currencies and two regions, where both regions run across countries.

He begins with the two countries, assuming that an asymmetric demand shock negatively affects country B: "To the extent that prices are allowed to rise in A, the change in the terms of trade will relieve B of some of the burden of adjustment." Ibid. (p. 658). However, it is possible that the unemployment pressure in B cannot be eased by increasing prices in A, if A's central bank will tighten credit to restrain inflationary pressure. Thus, the adjustment falls on B itself, if prices in B cannot decrease then the adjustment happens through decrease in employment.

He next discusses the impact of asymmetric demand shock on two regions in the same country. An asymmetric demand shock affects negatively region B. As a consequence, inflationary pressure occurs in A and creates unemployment pressure in B. The central bank can ease the pressure in B by increasing money supply in the country as a whole. This aggravates inflationary pressures in A, but may turn the terms of trade against B and correct the employment problem in B.

In the inter-regional adjustment the trade-off between inflation and unemployment ensures that unemployment in region B is prevented by the willingness of central bank to inflate in region A. In the inter-national example, unemployment in country B cannot be prevented as long as country A is unwilling to inflate. Mundell warns this logic only stretches so far, i.e. it does not follow that if the world consisted of one country with one currency that unemployment could be prevented by the pro-inflationary policies of a world central bank. The world as a whole is not an optimum currency area. If one considers the "inconvenience of money-changing" as the only cost of the existence of multiple currencies, then the world is an optimum currency area. With one world currency, the "inconvenience" disappears. Before OCA theory emerged, proponents of a single world currency frequently offered this argument. The Mundellian argument that the world is not an optimum currency area, in contrast, recognizes the stabilizing function of the exchange rate.

In the international adjustment example equilibrium could be returned with a depreciation in B and an appreciation in A. But one may ask whether flexible exchange rates help to ease the adjustment costs of asymmetric demand shock in all cases when national currencies are involved, in other words are optimum currency areas identical with countries? The argument for flexible exchange rates builds on the notion that people are unlikely to accept variation in their real income, or variations in the money wage or price level, yet readily accept variations in real income through changes in the rate of exchange. McKinnon (1963) develops this idea extensively.

Mundell responds that optimum currency areas are identical with economic regions, when defined by inter-regional labor mobility. Mundell defines region in terms of factor mobility. Internal factor mobility and external factor immobility characterize an economic region. In support of this argument, he brings up the third example of adjustment to asymmetric shock. Here, we assume two countries, the US and Canada and two regions East and West, so that the regions run across these countries. East in both countries produces timber, while West makes cars. As a result of an asymmetric shock, there is a pressure for unemployment in the East, which central banks in both countries attempt to relieve. This strengthens the inflationary pressures in the Western regions. If inflation is prevented in both countries, unemployment in both cannot be avoided. The reverse also applies. In this example, however, it is not clear which country should devalue, so flexible exchange rates do not necessarily bring back the equilibrium. Mundell concludes the two countries do not form optimum currency areas.

While this example weakens the case for the flexible exchange rates, the argument remains valid when currencies are organized at a regional, rather than national, basis. This is the core of Mundell's argument; flexible exchange rates between two countries are preferable to fixed exchange rates, unless the countries themselves do not form optimum currency areas.

If the sole goal pursued is economic stability, the greater the number of currency areas connected with flexible exchange rates the better. But should every little place with immobile labor be considered an optimum currency area with its own currency? Again, the answer is yes if stability (low adjustment costs to asymmetric shocks) is the sole criterion for judging the usefulness of a currency. Mundell writes, "...if then, the goals of internal stability are to be rigidly pursued, it follows that the greater is the number of separate currency areas in the world, the more successfully will these goals be attained." Mundell (1961, p. 662). However, if we consider the costs of having many currencies, some tradeoff must be found. Mundell sets forth an additional argument against an extremely large number of currency areas. Besides money-changing costs, a large number of currency areas mean that market for foreign exchange would be very thin. Moreover, in very small currency areas, imports are likely to play a huge role in regional consumption, which in turn weakens the possibility for money illusion.

In summary, the argument for flexible exchange rates rests on the closeness with which countries correspond to regions. If a nation is an economic region with internal factor mobility and external factor immobility, the argument for flexible exchange rates holds. If nations are dissimilar to regions, fixed exchange rates may do as well as flexible exchange rates. In Mundell's words,

"I have argued that the stabilization argument for flexible exchange rates is valid only if it is based on regional currency areas. If the world can be divided into regions within each of which there is factor mobility and between which there is factor immobility, then each of these regions should have a separate currency which fluctuates relative to all other currencies." ibid. (1961, p. 663).

Discussion of Mundell's Contribution

Mundell's seminal paper remains a pleasure to read. Mundel received the 1999 Nobel Prize for Economics "for his analysis of monetary and fiscal policy under different exchange rate regimes and his analysis of optimum currency areas." As with most frame-breaking contributions, it received a thorough peer review and raised several controversial points.

The first point of contention is Mundell's definition of region, which is neither geographical nor political. As Kenen (1969, p. 44) points out, "perfect interregional labor mobility requires perfect occupational mobility. And this can only come about when labor is homogenous." If one sticks to this interpretation of Mundell's original definition, an optimum currency area always has to be small. On the other hand, if there were perfect labor mobility around the world, a single currency would suffice for the whole world. Kenen (p.113) continues,

"We do not have perfect mobility because perfect interregional mobility implies perfect occupational mobility and the latter does not prevail. The labor force is not so homogeneous that it is possible to talk about perfect mobility, or even hope to delineate a region over which there is perfect mobility, unless that region is a single-product region."

McKinnon (1963) also qualifies Mundell's concept of labor mobility. If each region contains specialized industry, it may be difficult to distinguish between low geographic and low inter-industrial labor mobility. For example, if a negative asymmetric shock affects region B and there is a possibility in region B to develop A-type industries, the "need for factor movement between A and B is not great. ... But if B cannot easily develop A-type industries, then factor movements to A may be the only thing that will prevent a large fall in the unit incomes of potentially mobile factors of production in B." (p. 724)

Grubel (1970, p. 321) argues Mundell's definition of region is inapplicable to real world problems, because Mundell does not distinguish between different degrees of labor mobility. Grubel writes that Mundell's definition of regions, i.e. "regions are areas within which there is factor mobility, but between which there is factor immobility" (Mundell, 1961, p. 658) is too broad and has little practical application.

Giersch (1973) reasons that Mundell's concept of factor mobility implies that in the long run the world is an optimum currency area. In Mundell's view, labor mobility justifies fixed exchange rates, since sufficiently mobile labor weakens the need for flexible exchange rates. But "since mobility is a function of time and hence very high in the long run, even over large distances, the logical conclusion seems to be that in the long run the optimum currency area must be the whole world." Giersch (1973) also points out to situation in which migration could be the worst response to balance of payments adjustment since migration is very likely irreversible.

Corden (1973) is rather skeptical concerning the importance of labor mobility in the adjustment to asymmetric shocks. He writes,

"Can it really be imagined that a U.K. depressed-area problem could be solved by the large-scale migration of British workers to Germany? It is conceivable; but when Britons are reluctant even to move from Scotland or Tyneside to the south, though the language is almost the same, it takes some imagination to conceive of labor mobility solving the central problem of monetary integration." Corden (1973, p. 168).

Corden (1973, pp.168-169) argues that short-run capital mobility can be helpful, but in the long-run capital mobility cannot solve the adjustment problem for two countries affected by asymmetric shocks.

"No country or region can borrow indefinitely on a private market, however, open and efficient the market is, to sustain levels of real wages, and hence real consumption levels which are too high, bearing in mind the productivity of the country or region. ... Furthermore, as its debt obligations increase, the country will become less credit-worthy. Obviously, there is no long-term solution here. Of course, a country can borrow on the capital market indefinitely, or for long periods, if new productive investment opportunities are opening up, but that is another matter." Salant (1973, pp. 201-202) writes, "Corden's rationale for a deficit region not being able to borrow indefinitely to finance its deficit depends on the assumption that such borrowing absorbs an increasing proportion of financial resources available to the region from outside. This is not necessarily true in a growth situation; if the growth of financial resources available to the region is greater than the rate of growth of its borrowing, then the process could continue indefinitely."

Corden (1973) also argues that Mundell's adjustment mechanism impliedly assumes countries are on a wage standard, i.e. a country has a certain level of money wages that "together with levels and rates of increase in productivity, determine levels of monetary demand required for full employment. Appropriate monetary and fiscal policies are then implemented to validate the money wage level. The crucial assumption is that governments are committed to full employment and that money wages are not sufficiently flexible downwards."

Ingram (1969) notes that in defining regions Mundell emphasizes labor, instead of capital, mobility. He further argues that Mundell's analysis in a multi-region area leads to the conclusion that "when one region has unemployment, other regions will have to accept inflation in order to relieve the unemployment. Thus, we expect differing degrees of inflation in the regions." Ingram then adds that the empirical evidence does not apparently support this inference.

Melitz (1995) observes that "It would require a very restrictive macroeconomic model to conclude that geographical labor mobility between regions is the critical variable in adjusting to a trade shock. On the other hand, the assumption of no international labor mobility would obviously not yield the result that all countries are already optimal currency areas.... Of course, people change locations more readily within countries than between them. But whether they should also have a separate currency is precisely what the analysis of the optimum currency area is supposed to examine. The role of geographical labor mobility in any well-tested, well-specified theory of the optimum currency area remains to be seen." Melitz (1995, p. 499).

Bofinger (1994) counters Mundell's argument with an example that considers a country affected by a negative demand shocks to a good, which constitutes only a minor portion of country's production and which is not produced in other member-countries.

"In order to over come such a shock without undesired effects on output and employment, it would be necessary that the relative price of this good decreases (in comparison with all other goods be they produced abroad or at home). Under these assumptions the exchange rate would obviously be an inappropriate adjustment instrument, because it can only shift the whole price level of one country vis-à-vis the price level of another country. ...Thus, if economies are highly diversified, exchange rate changes have to be regarded as a therapy that is associated with very negative side effects." Bofinger (1994, p. 8). He further argues that thinking based on a "one-country, one-sector" model with an adjustment mechanism dependent on downward inflexibility of prices and wages and money illusion led economists to the fallacy that the nominal exchange rate is useful for changing relative prices. Furthermore, he sees as misplaced the emphasis on the real asymmetric shocks, since asymmetric monetary shocks have far wider reaching consequences for highly diversified economies.

There is also skepticism as to whether exchange rate adjustment to asymmetric shocks is the least costly way of adjustment in the case of sticky prices, low labor mobility and no fiscal transfers. De Grauwe (1994, pp. 37-44) summarizes some of the theoretical objection to this view: "In the long run nominal exchange rate changes do not affect the real exchange rate of a country. Structural differences should be tackled with structural policies. Manipulating money (its quantity or its price) cannot change these real differences."

Another argument may be made that devaluation does not always have a positive effect on output, and sometimes this effect is contractionary. Krugman and Taylor (1978) initiated the contractionary devaluation debate. For an excellent review, see Agenor and Montiel (1996). Furthermore, countries with firms that have large currency liabilities may force such firms into bankruptcy in the event of a large-scale devaluation (Calvo, 1999). Other researchers argue that the exchange rate follows a random walk, i.e. there is no reliable relation between fundamentals and exchange rates. Bofinger (1994, p. 11) puts it in a very direct way: "Therefore, the empirical evidence for a reliable reaction of flexible exchange rates to asymmetric real shocks is simply not existent."

Mundell's basic argument survives despite these valid criticisms. Mundell's labor mobility is today understood as a criterion of defining an optimum currency area. Even more in policy applications it is sometimes seen as if there would be a trade-off between the exchange rate flexibility and labor market flexibility. For example Gylfason (2002, p.1) writes, "... the crucial question of rigidity versus flexibility in our economic system is not confined to exchange rate regimes. No, I think we need to take a broad view of rigidity and flexibility, a view that incorporates labor market arrangements in particular." And on p. 5 "[O]ne of the main advantages of labor market flexibility is that it makes a nation free to choose between fixed and flexible exchange rates. Rigid labor markets tie the hands of nations: with rigid wages, fixed exchange rates can lead to persistent, even permanent unemployment and economic stagnation of the type that the United Kingdom experienced under the gold standard between the two world wars."

Subsequent research puts forward additional criteria, some of which I review below.

Degree of Openness

McKinnon (1963) considers the openness of economy, defined as the ratio of tradables to non-tradables, as the crucial criterion of optimality of currency areas. His argument is that the more open the economy, the more it will be inclined to use fixed exchange rates, i.e. flexible exchange rates are more advantageous for fairly closed economies.

Consider a small country in which the ratio of exportables, X_1 and importables, X_2 to non-tradables X_3 is rather high. Under flexible exchange rate arrangements price of exportables, P_1 and importables, P_2 expressed in domestic currency varies with the exchange rate, while P_3 may be assumed constant. Consequently, in small open economy, fluctuations in the exchange rate contradict to efforts to maintain stable price level. The picture is different in a large country with sizable production of non-tradable goods. The devaluation would have an effect on P_1 and P_2 but the effect on the general price index will be lower than in the case of small open economy. In McKinnon's words (p. 719), "...if we move across the spectrum from closed to open economies, flexible exchange rates become both less effective as a control device for external balance and more damaging to internal price level stability."

Thus, small open economies may find it beneficial to join larger currency areas. Ishiyama (1975) comments that similar results are obtained using foreign trade multiplier analysis with constant prices. Here openness would be measured as the ratio of trade to income. Thus, the more open the economy, the larger the variation in income under flexible exchange rates. Tower and Willett (1976) maintain the view that the benefits from a monetary union increase with the degree of openness.

McKinnon (1963) makes a case that economies with high ratio of tradables to non-tradables should rely more on fiscal and monetary policies than on exchange rates to cure the balance of payments disequilibra.

"When a trade deficit exists only a relatively small reduction in spending will be necessary to bring adjustment, when the economy is open. As exportables and importables are a large part of total spending, a relatively small reduction in demand, for example, would be sufficient to release exportables from domestic consumption and to reduce imports, thus improving the trade balance." Presley and Dennis (1976, p. 19).

Thus, small countries that trade extensively find it beneficial to form currency areas.

Ishiyama (1975) notes that McKinnon (1963) assumes that the outside world price level is stable. Otherwise, his argument could be completely reversed, since "external instability would be directly propagated to the domestic economy through fixed exchange." Giersch (1973) makes a similar point: the more open is the economy the more it may need exchange rate flexibility, since it may be more exposed to cyclical disturbances from the outside world from which it wants to isolate itself.

McKinnon (1963) raises another point which favors fixed exchange rates in small open economies: the higher probability of the absence of money illusion. The presence of money illusion is what allows flexible exchange rates to perform their stabilizing function. McKinnon argues the money illusion is lowest in highly open economies. In a dynamic framework, this argument is hardly valid. The more times the country devalues, the more likely the devaluation will have inflationary consequences, and therefore decrease the probability of a future devaluation. As Mundell (1997, p. 34) puts it, "The first devaluation may work without too much inflation; the second invites a wage response; and the third provokes compensation demands."

There is an additional argument that connects the size of a country with optimum currency area issues. In a large area, it may be easier to keep the value of money "in terms of a representative bundle of economic goods." "If the area under consideration is sufficiently large so that the body of non-tradable goods is large, then pegging the value of the domestic currency to this body of non-tradable goods is sufficient to give money liquidity value in the eyes of the inhabitants of the area in question." McKinnon (1963, p. 722).

Thus, the existence of stable large countries is required for small countries to efficiently peg their currencies. Bofinger (1994) raises an argument against small currency areas, whereby transferring monetary policy-making to supranational authorities decreases the influence of national politicians, i.e. the smaller the currency area, the more serious the political interference with monetary policy-making.

Degree of Product Diversification

Kenen (1969) suggests production diversification as a characteristic for optimum currency areas. He writes that a well-diversified economy will rarely confront changes in demand for its export products. "... a well diversified national economy will not have to undergo changes in its terms of trade as often as a single product national economy." Kenen

(1969, p. 49). In well-diversified economies, the importance of asymmetric shocks would be of lesser significance than in less-diversified economies.

"A country that engages in a number of activities is also apt to export a wide range of products. Each individual export may be subject to disturbances, whether due to changes in external demand or in technology. But if those disturbances are independent, consequent on variations in the composition of expenditure or output, rather than massive macroeconomic swings affecting the entire export array, the law of large numbers will come into play. At any point in time, a country can expect to suffer significant reversals in export performance, but also enjoy significant successes. ... From the standpoint of external balance, taken by itself, economic diversification, reflected in export diversification, serves, ex ante, to forestall the need for frequent changes in the terms of trade and therefore, for frequent changes in national exchange rates." (p. 49).

Kenen argues that product diversification decreases the likelihood of asymmetric shocks and alleviates their negative effects. Thus, fixed rates are "most appropriate – or least inappropriate – to well-diversified economies."

The core of this argument rests on the idea that "positive changes with respect to some exports will be offset by negative changes with respect to others; as demand for some increases, the demand for others falls. The more diversified are export products, the greater will be this offsetting mechanism." Presley and Dennis (1976, p. 24). A country that produces a wide variety of goods will experience a slower decrease in overall production, if in the outside markets the demand for its goods decreases. Thus, a country with a low degree of product diversification needs flexible exchange rates to cushion it from outside shocks, while a highly diversified economy may find it beneficial to form a currency area.

Mundell (1969, p. 111) responds that if one follows Kenen's criterion of the optimum currency area then "the most highly diversified economy is the world economy. Then, in terms of an insurance principle and from the point of view of hedging against risks of fluctuation, a world currency is the best solution."

McKinnon (1969, p. 112) makes another point.

"Kenen's main conclusion could be put as follows: the more diversified an economy the stronger the case for fixed exchange rates. However, the more diversified an economy, the larger it is, and, because it is diversified, the smaller the foreign trade sector. Therefore, Kenen's conclusions imply that a large diversified economy with a small foreign sector should have fixed exchange rates whereas small open economies should adhere to floating rates."

Melitz (1995, pp. 498-499) doubts Kenen's argumentation implies that a country with not diversified production structure benefits from exchange rate flexibility.

Policy Oriented Criteria

The above-mentioned contributions deal with criteria that depend on the state of the economy (labor mobility, openness, and product diversification). The discussion later moved toward criteria that depend on desired policy tradeoffs. Ishiyama (1975) reviews these criteria thoroughly, so I only mention those criteria that still seem to play a role in the discussion about monetary integration. These include similarity of rates of inflation, degree of policy integration, degree of price and wage flexibility, and real exchange rate variability.

If the criterion is the similarity of inflation rates, then the concept is simple: it is difficult to fix an exchange rate if one country inflates and the other does not. Fleming (1971) notes a danger in the fixed exchange rate area originating from "the relative cost levels of the participating countries [being] out of line." Fleming (1971, p. 468). In Fleming's view, this can happen when there are differences among countries in unemployment preferences, in productivity growth rates and/or in trade union aggressiveness. He also points to the danger that being in a fixed exchange rate area may force a country to accept a higher level of unemployment and a lower rate of inflation "that would correspond to their preferred compromise between the two." (p. 468) Haberler (1970) raises the point that it is not the characteristics of the economy, but the similarity of policy attitudes, which creates the conditions for a flourishing currency area. Fleming (1971) argues that flexible adjustment of prices and wages to excess demand and excess supply would bring automatic adjustment to asymmetric shocks, so the need for exchange rate adjustment simply would not be there. If real exchange rate adjustment is needed, it does not matter whether the required adjustment will happen through prices, wages, or exchange rates. However, collective bargaining, monopolistic and oligopolistic markets, and natural or state-induced monopolies reduce the extent of wage and price flexibility. Vaubel (1990) proposes the real exchange rate as an optimum currency area characteristic, arguing that it is a more comprehensive criterion than the traditional criteria of labor mobility, diversification, and openness.

Political Commitment to Exchange Rate Decisions

A part of the OCA literature posits that an optimum currency area may be more about long-term political commitment than economic criteria. Ingram (1969) claims that economic considerations take a back seat in choosing exchange rate arrangements, so it is somewhat futile to stress definitions of optimal currency area characteristics. What matters is a government's commitment to such a decision.

"It seems to me that the geographic extent of a currency area ... can be whatever we want it to be, large or small, although I do agree that when the currency area becomes very small we lose the advantages of the use of money. I do not think the optimum size of a currency area can be discovered by looking for real economic determinants of it, such as degree of labor mobility or homogeneity of output, although these factors may certainly affect the speed and ease of adjustment. I think the efficacy of a currency area depends on policy positions taken by governments and on the firmness of their commitment to them, on attitudes of the population toward the adjustment processes involved, on the nature of financial and other institutions, and on some economic considerations that are largely omitted from much present analysis." Ingram (1969, pp. 97-98).

Mintz (1970) also emphasizes the political willingness of the central authorities to pursue monetary unions as the most important factor for forming currency areas.

Along similar lines, Machlup (1977, p. 71) argues:

"What ultimately counts, however, is that all members are willing to give up their independence in matters of money, credit, and interest. Pragmatically, therefore, an optimum currency area is a region no part of which insists on creating money and having a monetary policy of its own."

This seems to be the opinion also of some authors in the 1990s. Goodhart (1995) argues that any currency union formation is primarily governed by political concerns. Goodhart (1996) writes about EMU aspirations: "I shall argue that attempting to fix even more rigid, and supposedly irrevocable, currency linkages in advance of, and in the absence of, political and fiscal cohesion among the member states, is also a dangerous exercise." (p. 1084).

Goodhart continues, "What is clear is that currency union is essentially a function of political cohesion." In this context, Bean (1992) and Feldstein (1997) argue along a similar line.

Recent Developments in OCA Theory

International macroeconomics has gone through substantial changes in the last two decades. These changes are reflected in the discussion on optimum currency area theory and in discussions on choosing an optimal exchange rate regime. A crucial change has occurred since the early 1960s in the understanding of the inflation-unemployment trade-off as confidence in permanent trade-off have broken down. Niehans (1984) calls it an elimination of the 'Phillips illusion' from national monetary policy. Tavlas (1993) says OCA theory has largely been modified as the discussion has turned to expectation formation, credibility, and time inconsistency. For example, time inconsistency suggests that inflation may increase if policy-makers and wage-setters engage in a game. See Barro and Gordon (1983). The costs of decreasing inflation are also lowered as the credibility of the central bank increases. A traditionally high inflation country can gain credibility by "tying its hands," i.e. pegging its exchange rate to a low inflation country. Thus, joining a currency union provides an important benefit to a potential member-country.

"The surrender of all national monetary policy responsibilities to a supranational central bank system is the most obvious signal that a country is no longer attempting to make use of surprise inflation. Of course, this requires that the central bank which in charge of the common currency has a higher credibility than the national central bank." Bofinger (1994, p. 21). In the same paper, Bofinger labels capital movements unconnected to macroeconomic fundamentals as asymmetric and makes an argument that "the complete avoidance of such [asymmetric monetary] shocks constitutes a very fundamental benefit of any monetary union." (p. 25) Furthermore, he makes a case in favor of larger currency areas, arguing that money demand is more stable in large currency areas, since "intra-regional shifts occurring within a common currency area only affect the regional money demand functions but not the national demand function." (p. 26)

One can see the discussion on the optimum currency areas as a part of the problem of how to choose optimum exchange rate regime. It should be noted, however, that OCA theory is typically concerned with the choice between the pure float and fixed exchange rate regime, while the economic policy-making is usually concerned with the subtler problem of choosing among intermediary types of regimes. Apart from the attitude rooted in the classical theory of optimum currency areas, one can distinguish three approaches in the literature on the search for an optimum exchange rate regime. The first approach considers a macroeconomic model and evaluates which exchange rate regime could ease the response of the economy to different disturbances. Aizenman and Flood (1992) present a two-country, one-good, one-factor model with nominal wage rigidities. Productivity shocks in this model hit asymmetrically the two member-countries of a currency union. Migration brings efficient adjustment through equalizing the marginal productivity of labor across both countries. The model of Aizenman and Flood (1992) accentuates the insight that under sticky wages and low labor mobility, a floating exchange rate may help the economy toward an efficient allocation of resources. Thus, a country exposed to external nominal shocks should typically use flexible rates to insulate its domestic economy. On the other hand, a fixed regime can be useful when dealing with domestic nominal shocks, while domestic real shocks are best handled under a flexible regime. See Argy (1990) for a review of this literature.

Buiter (1995) presents a thorough analytical discussion of the theoretical issues of forming currency areas in the context of a seven-equation model of what he terms a "semi-small" open economy with perfect capital mobility. In this model, Buiters distinguishes the character of shocks that affect the economy. He identifies an important role for nominal exchange rate flexibility in adjustment to real shocks. In the case of financial shocks, however, the model indicates that exchange rate flexibility is undesirable. Real shocks are "IS" shocks, shocks to the private or public demand for goods and services, while financial shocks are for example liquidity preference (money demand) shocks or shocks to the domestic money supply process. "Nominal exchange rate flexibility will cause financial shocks and other nominal shocks to result in temporary changes in international relative prices and costs – changes that are unnecessary and harmful from the point of view of the underlying real fundamentals and that involve real, albeit transitory, adjustment costs." (p. 23).

The second approach deals with the problem of the exchange rate regime in the context of stabilization plans. This approach considers a country with high inflation that wishes to stabilize with minimal costs of adjustment. As Bruno (1991) shows, in the absence of money illusion, the neutrality of money, as well as nominal-real dichotomy the general equilibrium analysis determines a unique solution for the real variables. The price level, however, remains indeterminate unless another nominal variable is fixed, i.e. correction of fundamentals is usually insufficient. Bruno (1991) argues that what needs to be done first is to remove the real source of the disequilibrium. However, it may happen that the correction of the macroeconomic fundamentals will not suffice to eliminate inflation. Inflation has a life of its own, i.e. a corrected real system can be consistent with more than one inflation rate. If, say, wages are backward indexed, i.e. even if inflation stops, lagged indexation may cause a large increase in real wages. In that case, the past is not forgotten. Now, even if the economy is de-indexed, there is still the problem of the credibility of the authorities, who are attempting to decrease inflation. Thus, a clearly identifiable nominal anchor must be introduced to signal of a shift in policy. For this reason, a clear signal (such a firm nominal anchor) of a shift in policy is needed. In a closed economy, the typical nominal anchor is the level of the money supply or in some cases nominal wage. In the open economy, the exchange rate is another possible nominal anchor. In the 1990s, country-specific discussions of optimum exchange rate regimes were, to a large extent, framed in this context, particularly in transition economies. See e.g. Guitián (1994), Bofinger, Flassbeck and Hoffmann (1997), and Horvath and Jonas (1999).

As the third approach, I consider modern theoretical contributions in the context of general-equilibrium models and based on microeconomic foundations. For an excellent detailed review of these contributions see Lafrance and St-Amant (1999). Helpman (1981) and Kareken and Wallace (1981) show that in an environment where asset markets are complete and money is neutral, the exchange rate regime has no social welfare impact. Helpman (1981) concludes that the method for choosing among different exchange rate regimes depends on the given rigidities and imperfections.

"There are various rigidities and imperfections (e.g. wage contracts, market imperfection) whose existence may have a bearing on the relative desirability of alternative exchange-rate regimes. Thus, it is possible that a particular exchange-rate regime performs better than others under certain types of imperfections. A characterization of imperfections under which each exchange-rate regime performs best will be valuable." Helpman (1981, p. 887). Kareken and Wallace (1981) indeterminacy result about the equilibrium exchange rates may be interpreted in the similar way.

The question thus becomes which regime is preferable under a given type of friction. Subsequent work introduces various rigidities and imperfections into the modeling of currency areas. Bayoumi (1994) and Ricci (1997) represent the literature in which wage and price rigidities are the frictions, while in Helpman and Razin (1982), and in Neumeyer (1998) the nature of the friction is represented by financial market incompleteness.

Helpman and Razin (1982) in a two-period general equilibrium model show that the incompleteness of financial markets is complemented by channels through which nominal variables have real effects, which allow them to provide a set of sufficient conditions under which a floating regime is preferred to a fixed regime. In their model, a floating exchange rate regime dominates a fixed regime, since the latter reduces the number of assets in the economy.

Bayoumi (1994) presents a model with regionally differentiated goods in which wages are downwardly rigid. Each region can choose to have its own currency or join a union. He presents a framework that allows him to incorporate several typical OCA factors as the size and correlation of the disturbances, the costs of transactions between different currencies, the level of factor mobility across regions and the inter-relationship of demand among regions. However, Bayoumi (1994) assigns no role for financial assets or government policy; in his model, each region is fully specialized in production of one specific good.

Bayoumi (1994, p. 552) then makes the surprising insight: "A currency union can raise the welfare of the regions within the union, it unambiguously lowers welfare for regions outside the union. This is because the gains from the union, in the form of lower costs of transacting business, are limited to the members of the union, while the losses from the union, in the form of lower output due to the interaction between the common exchange rate and the nominal rigidity, affect everybody." However, as Bayoumi himself writes, this result is model dependent. One can therefore imagine circumstances in which a currency union benefits those outside the union.

Another insight from Bayoumi (1994) concerns the fact that the incentives for a region to join a currency union may be different from the incentives to admit a region into a currency union. Bayoumi (1994, p. 552) next states the reasons: "The entrant gains from lower transaction costs on trade with the entire existing union, while the incumbent regions only gain on their trade with the potential entrant. As a result, a small region will always have a greater incentive to join a union than the union will have an incentive to admit the new member. A corollary of this is that, even if a country would prefer a free float across all regions, it may still have an incentive to join a currency union with other regions if it is going to be formed."

Ricci (1997) presents a model of optimum currency areas in a two-country trade regime with nominal rigidities that allows for consideration of monetary and real variables. Preferences differ in the two countries, which makes it possible to analyze the degree-of-openness effect and symmetry of shocks in the creation of currency unions. In his model, the net benefits from participation in a currency union increase with the following variables: the correlation of real shocks between countries, the degree of adjustment of labor and fiscal policy instruments, the difference between the inflationary bias of the domestic monetary authority and that of the currency union, the variability of domestic monetary shocks (which, in part, are transmitted to other countries inside the currency union), and the size of efficiency losses eliminated through the adoption of a common currency. Those factors that tend to diminish the benefits of monetary union include the variability of real and foreign monetary shocks and the correlation of monetary shocks between countries. In contrast to prevailing OCA opinion, Ricci (1997) shows ambiguous effects for the degree of openness when both real and monetary shocks are taken into account.

Canzoneri and Rogers (1990) develop a two-country model similar to the cash-in-advance model of Lucas and Stokey (1987). In this model, they consider the issue of the optimum currency area from the perspective of public finance. The optimal spreading of tax distortions may require different inflation in different regions, so each region would need its own currency to have its own inflation. They provide a formal definition of the optimum currency area problem: the policy-maker must choose the optimal number of currencies to maximize the weighted sum of the utilities of households of the two countries.

In a general equilibrium model with incomplete asset markets, nominal securities and mean-variance preferences, Neumeyer (1998) shows that adoption of a currency union is the result of a trade-off between the benefits of reducing excessive volatility of exchange rates and the costs of reducing the number of assets in the economy. Neumeyer (1998) differentiates between the economic and political shocks. While the fluctuation in exchange rates that reflect economic shocks may seem excessive, they help allocate resources efficiently. On the other hand, exchange rate volatility caused by non-economic (political) shocks reduces the efficiency of financial market. Neumeyer (1998, p. 246) writes that "Political interference in monetary affairs implies that given the realization of an economic shock, there still is uncertainty about the future actions of monetary authorities since such actions will be influenced by future political events. For example, the timing of monetary stabilizations in inflationary economies, the value at which currencies enter a fixed exchange rate regime, and exchange rate realignments are instances of monetary policy decisions that depend on the realization of political shocks."

He argues interestingly that "currency unions and permanently fixed exchange rate regimes can be viewed as monetary rules that attempt to improve welfare by insulating money from domestic politics." Neumeyer (1998, p. 247). On the other hand, fluctuation in the value of money reflecting economic shocks maybe "good," as it increases the insurance opportunities available through trade in nominal assets. As he puts it, "the loss of monetary independence ... is socially costly because it makes the real payoff of assets denominated in different currencies equivalent, effectively reducing the number of financial instruments with which economic agents can share risks." Neumeyer (1998, p. 247). The main result of Neumeyer (1998) is that adoption of a common currency increases welfare when the gain from "eliminating excess monetary volatility exceeds the cost of reducing the number of financial instruments in the economy."

Endogeneity Problem

Frankel and Rose (1997) build an argument that the international trade pattern and international business-cycle correlation is endogenous, i.e. countries with closer trade links tend to have more tightly correlated business cycles. Frankel and Rose (1997, p. 4) propose that "the more highly correlated the business cycles are across member countries, the more appropriate a common currency." If shocks are not correlated, but the cycle is correlated between two countries, then, most likely, the propagation mechanism transfers idiosyncratic shocks into positive co-movements of real variables. In their opinion, joining a currency union moves countries closer to meeting the optimum currency area criteria. In other words, "a naïve examination of historical data gives a misleading picture of a country's suitability for entry into a currency union, since the OCA [optimum currency area] criteria are endogenous."(p. 2) Entering a monetary union increases the symmetry in the business cycle of the prospective member-country due to common monetary policy and closer international trade ties. Frankel and Rose (1997) argue that the relationship between international trade and symmetry of business cycles is primarily an empirical one. If a closer trade relationship results in countries being more specialized, then one should expect more idiosyncratic cycles. If a closer trade relationship results in an increase in intra-industry trade, then cycles may become less idiosyncratic. The authors present empirical evidence supporting the latter view.

Corsetti and Pesenti (2002) take the endogeneity argument a step further. They use a general-equilibrium two-country, choice-theoretic, stochastic setting with imperfect competition in production, nominal rigidities in the goods markets and forward-looking price-setting by firms. They show that common monetary policy can be self-validating, "when the private sector chooses pricing strategies that are optimal in a monetary union, such strategies make a currency area the optimal monetary regime from the vantage point of the national policymakers as well. In other words, there is no incentive for monetary authorities to pursue independent strategies of national output stabilization. As a result, even if there is no structural change in fundamentals (e.g. no increase in intra-industry trade), national outputs become more correlated."(p. 2)

All in all, "the best institutional device to guarantee a credible policy commitment to a monetary union is to have the monetary union itself in place." (p. 22)

Empirical Evidence on Optimum Currency Areas

I review some of the empirical evidence presented in the literature, which in some way was written in the context of OCA theory. I begin with a snapshot of OCA studies and the world and then take a more detailed look at optimal currency areas in Western and transitional Europe. For analysis of shocks outside Europe, see Bayoumi and Eichengreen (1994), Horvath and Grabowski (1997), Grabowski and Horvath (1999), Yuen (2000), Mkenda (2001), and Grandes (2003).

OCA and the World

Ghosh and Wolf (1994) find little correlation between geographical proximity and the grouping of countries into optimum currency areas. Thus, their model suggests that restricting monetary unions into geographically neighboring areas implies high costs. Their results also suggest that adopting a single currency is very costly for most regions in the world and that most of the stabilization benefits across regions can be captured by a relatively small number of currencies. Their results further indicate that adopting a single currency around the world may be prohibitively costly, and imply that neither Europe nor the United States form an optimum currency area, because, for both regions, the costs of adopting a single currency exceeds estimates of the transaction cost savings. For example, they argue that for the US, G-7 or western European countries maintaining a single currency would amount (or amounts to) around 2.5% of GDP yearly (ignoring the transactions benefits). "With five currencies among the fifty US states, and three currencies among the twelve European Union countries, the stabilization costs fall to less than 1.5% of GDP. For other regions we consider, the CFA countries, the states of the former Soviet Union, and the world at large, the costs of adopting a single currency are significantly higher." Finally, they argue that there is no advantage for Germany and the United States to join any monetary union.

Artis, Kohler and Melitz (1998) taking two criteria of OCA literature (high level of bilateral trade and symmetry of shocks) identify four large optimum currency areas in the world, "Of these four large union, one covers virtually all of Western Europe; a second encompasses all of Mesoamerica and the Northern ridge of South America; a third occupies a good part of the Middle East, and a fourth englobes the entire ASEAN area, including China and Australia." Unlike Ghosh and Wold (1994), their program for finding optimum currency areas "displays a marked tendency to identify monetary unions on a geographical basis." (p. 27)

OCA and Western Europe

I next consider the exposure of an area to different shocks, and, to a lesser extent, the question of labor mobility and production diversification.

Asymmetric Shocks

The emphasis on asymmetric (country-specific) shocks is natural, since it seems that these shocks represent a crucial component in the choice of the exchange rate regime as viewed from the optimum currency area perspective. Is Western Europe a region where country-specific, idiosyncratic shocks prevail, or it is a region where shocks affect all the countries similarly? The earliest papers to tackle this issue were written in the late 1980s. Cohen and Wyplosz (1989), Weber (1990), and the EC Commission (1990) were the first to attempt to measure the symmetry of shocks in Europe.

Bayoumi and Eichengreen (1992) performed measurement of the incidence of shocks using a structural vector auto-regressive model in an effort to identify supply and demand shocks influencing output fluctuations in EC and some US regions in the period 1960-88. Minford (1993, pp. 236-237) argued that what their structural vector-autoregressive model really obtains is not the demand and supply shocks, but permanent and temporary shocks in terms of their effect on output. Buiter (1995, p. 28) writes that it is not sufficient to "identify demand and supply shocks and decompose them into idiosyncratic vs. common shocks. Demand shocks in turn have to be decomposed into financial (or LM) and goods market (or IS) shocks for it to be possible to draw sensible inferences about the appropriate exchange rate regime." Bayoumi and Eichengreen (1992) measure how the supply and demand shocks of different countries in the EC and different regions of the US correlate with benchmark regions (Germany for Europe and the mid-Atlantic for the United States). For Europe, they identify a core and periphery, based on the idea that if the country belongs to the core, then its shocks are correlated with the shocks to Germany. As Table 1 below indicates, supply shocks are highly correlated with Germany in such countries as France, Denmark, Belgium, and the Netherlands, while for other countries (England, Portugal, Ireland, Spain, Greece, and Italy) the correlation is lower. In this respect the situation in the United States regions is rather similar. There are regions with high correlation with the anchor region, the core, and regions with lower correlation, the periphery. However, the economic weight of the European periphery is greater. There is a noticeable difference between the correlation of demand shocks with the anchor region in the US and Europe. In Europe the correlation of demand shocks in EC countries with demand shocks of Germany is very low (higher for Denmark, France and Belgium, almost zero for Greece, Italy and Netherlands, and a slight negative correlation for Ireland and Spain). Bean (1992, p. 37) provides an interesting conjecture concerning the lower correlation of shocks in Europe relative to the US. "One would expect the cross-country correlation of demand shocks to be lower in Europe than in the United States, because there were periods in the sample when European countries pursued largely independent monetary policies and because the federal income tax and social security system in the United States ensures that the fiscal shocks are correlated across regions." Bayoumi and Eichengreen (1993) extend this analysis to the EFTA countries and show that Austria, Sweden, and Switzerland also belong to the European core.

Chamie, DeSerres and Lalonde (1994) decompose shocks to real supply, real demand, and nominal shocks in a vector auto-regressive system using the growth rates of output, prices, and money. They obtain monetary shocks by imposing the restriction of long-term money neutrality. Their results indicate that in Europe only Germany and Switzerland are strongly related to the symmetrical component of shocks. Other countries (Greece, Italy, Norway, Portugal, and Sweden) are not statistically related to the common component of the shocks. Also relative to US regions, these countries face highly asymmetric supply and real demand shocks. From this, they deduce that some European countries could face significant adjustment costs when joining a monetary union.

Whitt (1995) obtained supply and demand shocks from different data than Bayoumi and Eichengreen (1992). Instead of real GDP and GDP deflator he used monthly data for industrial production and price index. His analysis indicates that only France, Italy, and the Netherlands show substantial positive correlation of shocks with the anchor region (Germany). He also concludes that Canada and the United States may be the best candidates for monetary union, since they exhibit substantial positive supply and demand shocks.

Bayoumi and Prasad (1995) compare eight US regions with eight Western European countries. They find that "the relative importance of aggregate, industry-specific, and country- or region-specific shocks in explaining output growth fluctuations is roughly similar in Europe and the United States, with each of these types of shocks playing an important role." (p. 22)

Dibooglu and Horvath (1997) identify the shocks as supply, nominal, and real fiscal. Using data for 20 European market economies, they compare original members of the European Community to new members and non-members. Shocks are mostly country-specific, particularly for newer members and non-members, suggesting the importance of alternative adjustment mechanisms other than national monetary policies after the introduction of a single currency. Funke (1997) shows that the correlation of shocks among the EU countries is much lower than within Germany. Lafrance and St-Amant (1999, p. 7) comment on these empirical results: "Although the contemporaneous correlation of shocks might be relatively low, the two economies could still be in similar positions in the business cycle and not require divergent monetary policies or an exchange rate adjustment. On the other hand, while the correlation of shocks might be very high, the transmission mechanisms might be sufficiently different to justify an exchange rate adjustment." Willett (2001, p. 14) critically asserts that "simple statistical tests of past patterns of shocks, despite their recent popularity in the literature, are unlikely by themselves to offer good guidance to future patterns of shocks." Boone (1997) questions the exogeneity of these shocks by arguing that parameters change over time. Melitz and Weber (1996) examined the correlation of the structural components of output, and found more symmetry between the French and German economies than was typically found by structural shocks. Table 1 below compares these results.

Table 1. Shocks between Germany and Western European Countries

	Supply Shocks			Demand Shocks			Fiscal Shocks
	A	B	C	A	B	C	C
France	0.54	0.26	0.37	0.35	0.14	0.07	0.37
United Kingdom	0.11	0.45	0.36	0.16	0.31	0.00	0.11
Italy	0.23	-0.05	0.35	0.17	-0.28	0.09	0.38
Netherlands	0.59	0.51	0.45	0.17	0.47	0.32	0.05
Belgium	0.61	0.40	0.21	0.33	0.18	0.04	0.20
Denmark	0.59	0.31	0.42	0.39	0.24	-0.04	-0.13
Ireland	-0.06	-0.04	0.07	-0.08	0.16	-0.09	0.12
Spain	0.31	-0.25	-0.02	-0.07	0.10	-0.12	-0.01
Portugal	0.21	0.14	0.01	0.21	0.22	-0.02	-0.07
Greece	0.14	0.21	0.13	0.19	0.22	0.15	0.08
Austria		0.62	-0.26		0.34	0.17	0.12
Finland		0.22	0.12		-0.01	0.11	0.00
Norway		-0.06	-0.25		0.12	0.22	0.16
Sweden		0.35	0.20		-0.09	0.26	-0.01

Results of structural vector autoregressive estimations
Sources: A. Bayoumi and Eichengreen (1992) based on yearly data for the period 1960-1988.
B. Funke (1997) based on yearly data for the period 1964-1992.
C. Dibooglu and Horvath (1997) based on yearly data for the period 1950-1994.

These measurements, which focus on the contemporaneous correlation of shocks, appear to indicate that symmetry prevails for a sub-group of countries. It also appears that asymmetry prevails for some countries at the geographical periphery. Goodhart (1996) writes: "There is, however, a reasonable case that some of the core countries of north-west Europe are so alike in structure, facing similar shocks, with inter-twined economies, that a single central policy would closely mimic their preferred national policies. But that is hardly the case for the peripheral countries in Europe." (p. 1086)

Supply and Demand Shocks: Methodology

The classical paper on the optimum currency area by Mundell (1961) emphasizes the importance of retaining exchange rate flexibility in countries facing asymmetric demand shocks, particularly if these countries are unable to adjust otherwise due to wage rigidity, non-existent fiscal transfers and limited labor mobility. In this respect the evaluation of the costs of joining a currency union is connected with the identification of the character of shocks affecting a given area. Mundell's argument sends the following warning: if shocks affecting countries are symmetric then joining a currency union will not constrain, since for symmetric shocks an overall union response will suffice. If, on the other hand, the shocks are mainly asymmetric then an over-all response can do more harm than good, implying that the joining of a currency union could be costly.

There is no unique way of identifying different shocks affecting a given economy. Typically authors follow a strategy suggested by Bayoumi and Eichengreen (1992), where the identification strategy is based on a simple aggregate supply/aggregate demand model with a positively sloped short run, and a vertical long run aggregate supply curve. In this framework, the demand shocks only have transitory effects on output.

Consider two types of orthogonal shocks that are the sources of variation in domestic output, y_t, and the price level, p_t: a supply shock, ε_{1t}, and a demand shock, ε_{2t}.

Assuming that the vector $\Delta X_t = [\Delta y_t\ \Delta p_t]$ is stationary and can be written as an infinite moving average process:

$$\Delta x_t = \sum_{i=0}^{\infty} A_i \varepsilon_{t-i} = A(L)\varepsilon_t \quad \text{or}$$

$$\begin{pmatrix} \Delta y_t \\ \Delta p_t \end{pmatrix} = \begin{pmatrix} a_{11}(L) a_{12}(L) \\ a_{21}(L) a_{22}(L) \end{pmatrix} \begin{pmatrix} \varepsilon_{1t} \\ \varepsilon_{2t} \end{pmatrix}$$

where $a_{ij}(L)$ are polynomials and A_i are matrices in the lag operator L. The time paths of the effects of various shocks on the growth rate of output and prices are given by the coefficients of the polynomials $a_{ij}(L)$. Furthermore, coefficient $a_{ij}(k)$ in the $a_{ij}(L)$ polynomial is the response of variable i to a unit shock in ε_{it} after k periods. We also adopt the notation such that $a_{ij}(1)$ is the sum of all the moving average coefficients and gives the cumulative effect of ε_{jt} on variable i over time. The shocks have the following properties: the variance is normalized to equal unity, $E(\varepsilon_t\varepsilon_t') = I$, $E(\varepsilon_t, \varepsilon_{t+j}) = 0$, and $\forall j \neq 0$.

In order to identify this model, one can estimate a finite order bivariate VAR

$$\Delta x_t = b_1 \Delta x_{t-1} + b_2 \Delta x_{t-2} + \ldots b_k \Delta x_{t-k} + e_t$$

where the maximum lag length k is chosen such that residuals e_{it}, approximate white noise and

$$E(e_t e_t') = \Sigma = \begin{pmatrix} \sigma_{11}\sigma_{12} \\ \sigma_{21}\sigma_{22} \end{pmatrix}$$

Since the elements of ΔX_t are stationary, the system can be inverted to obtain the moving average representation:

$$\Delta x_t = e_t + c_1 e_{t-1} + c_2 e_{t-2} + \ldots = \sum_{i=0}^{\infty} c_i e_{t-i} = C(L) e_t$$

The contemporaneous relationship between the orthogonal (pure) innovations ε_t and the composite innovations e_t is

$$e_t = A_0 \varepsilon_t$$

Thus the following relationship exists between the variance-covariance matrices:

$$E(e_t e_t') = A_0 E(\varepsilon_t \varepsilon_t') A_0'$$

And

$$\Sigma = A_0 A_0'$$

Σ is a symmetric matrix with known elements, which imposes one restriction on the matrix of contemporaneous effects, A_0, which has four elements. Additional restrictions are needed to identify A_0, so that the orthogonal shocks ε_{it} can be recovered. Blanchard and Quah (1989) concentrate on the relationship between the matrices of long term effects. Then

$$A(1) = C(1) A_0$$

where C(1) contains known elements. In order to identify the shocks, we impose the following restriction on the long run matrix A(1): the aggregate supply curve is vertical in the long run. This corresponds to the restriction that $a_{12}(1) = 0$. After A_0 is identified, one can recover the orthogonal shocks.

As a final result of estimation we obtain for each country two series of exogenous shocks: supply shock, $\varepsilon_{1,t,p}$, and demand shock, $\varepsilon_{2,t,p}$, where p is the number of countries. Then correlation of these shocks is computed between countries.

Labor Mobility and Product Diversification

One important message of OCA theory is that countries affected by asymmetric shocks need substantial flexibility in their labor markets. A high degree of labor mobility may serve as a channel through which adjustment to shocks occurs.

Blanchard and Katz (1992) present empirical evidence that labor mobility in the United States has played an important role in adjustment, substituting to a large extent for price flexibility. Masson and Taylor (1994) compare the dispersion of unemployment rates across both the US and Canadian regions with European countries. Their results show that dispersion of unemployment is lowest in the US, higher in Canada, and highest in European countries. In Europe, the higher dispersion of unemployment rates reflects the fact that migration among European countries is clearly lower than among US regions or Canadian provinces. Labor mobility in the United States is roughly two to three times higher than in Europe; Masson and Taylor (1994, p. 25).

De Grauwe and Vanhaverbeke (1991) measure regional and national labor mobility across several western European countries. They show that the yearly flow of migrants among

EC countries is less than one tenth of the yearly flow of migrants between regions. They compare the nature of the adjustment to shocks between regions of the same country and between countries in Europe by computing different measures of real exchange rate variability for different regions and countries for the period 1977-85. They observe, "The variability of the real exchange rates of nations is about twice as large as the one observed at the regional level." (p. 4) The variability was lower in the EMS countries than in non-EMS countries. Southern countries had a much lower degree of interregional mobility than core countries, even if in Southern countries the regional differences in per capita income were higher than in the core.

Bayoumi and Prasad (1995) investigate the degree of labor market integration for eight US regions and eight EU countries. Their results indicate that the region-specific shocks are more important in the non-traded goods sector in the US, while in the EU country-specific shocks prevail in the traded goods sectors. The US has a more integrated labor market, and in Europe labor flows do not seem to facilitate adjustment.

Fatas (1997) uses employment growth rates to approximate business cycle movements and presents results, which indicate "national borders have seen their economic significance reduced over time as the process of integration has increased cross-border correlations and reduced within-border comovements." (p. 743) Puhani (1999) estimates the elasticity of migration with respect to changes in unemployment and income on the basis of regional panel data for Germany, France and Italy. His results show that the labor mobility is the highest in Germany, followed by France and Italy, but even in Germany the accommodation of a shock to unemployment by migration takes several years. Puhani (1999) concludes, "Labor mobility is extremely unlikely to act as a sufficient adjustment mechanism to asymmetric shocks in Euroland."

Buiter (1995) questions the relevance of these endeavors: "While it is correct that the US has more mobile labour than the EU, I would argue that even the US does not have the kind and degree of inter-state labour mobility that would be required to make up for the loss of an independent currency. The international factor mobility that is required to compensate fully for the loss of the ability to vary the nominal exchange rate, is a strictly temporary (that is reversible) migration. The fact that there is little or no permanent international migration among the EU member states is irrelevant from the point of view of EMU, just as the fact that there is rather more permanent or long-term inter-state labour mobility in the USA is irrelevant to the issue as to whether or not the USA is an optimal currency area. Permanent international factor mobility is not a substitute for nominal exchange rate flexibility." (pp. 30-31)

One may argue as Krugman (1993) that greater integration among countries and regions increases their specialization and thus the potential for asymmetric shocks. The counter-argument here stresses that greater integration increases intra-industry trade and thus the possibility for symmetry of shocks. This argument would be more in line with the message of Kenen (1969). European Commission (1990) also argues that in the future European Monetary Union a reduction of asymmetries between member countries may be expected. Kim (1997) brings evidence about long-run trends in regional specialization in the United States for the period 1840-1987. Prior to the early twentieth century, regional specialization was on the rise; but since the 1950s, the decreased significance of agriculture and manufacturing and the rising importance of the third sector have led to convergence in regional economic structures. Fontagne and Freudenberg (1999) distinguish between horizontally differentiated goods (two-way trade in varieties) and vertically differentiated products (two-way trade in different qualities). They show that only a part of intra-industry trade will increase symmetry of shocks, because "a distinction must be made between greater horizontal and vertical differentiation of production: growth in the latter process is not necessarily associated with more symmetric shocks." Their empirical evidence, however, favors the view that "the empirical evidence of structural asymmetries between core and periphery countries no longer justifies fears of cumulative divergence between members, within the EMU." (p. 279)

In summary one can probably say that the message of the optimum currency area literature is as follows: "There are costs and benefits to both fixed and flexible exchange rate regimes and [that] these may vary substantially across countries based on a number of characteristics." Willett and Wihlborg (1999, p. 61). Fixed exchange rates or a single currency may be more efficient than a flexible exchange rate arrangement for a small, open country with diversified production structure and integrated within a given geographic area in factor mobility. Tavlas (1993). The criteria suggested in the OCA literature give no clear-cut guidance for choosing an exchange rate regime. Moreover, political factors seem to play important role in such decisions. The theoretical considerations stemming from OCA theory are not easily translated into practical procedures. Masson and Taylor (1993, pp.17-18) also write, "there is no single over-riding criterion that could be used to assess the desirability or viability of a currency union." Nevertheless, this theory and its modifications form the intellectual foundation of any discussion on currency unions. Concurring with Willett (2001), I conclude that optimum currency area theory is essentially an approach to thinking about exchange rate regimes. As such, one should not expect it to produce any single quantifiable criterion. Swoboda (1999) also considers OCA theory "an analytical framework" for debates on creation of currency unions.

Exchange Rate Arrangements and Macroeconomic Performance

Schumpeter (1954) in Chapter on *Value and Money* discusses the impact of domestic and international monetary affairs on the real economy. He contrasts monetary with real analysis, and sees important links between international monetary affairs and the creation of wealth in general. He writes (p.277) that "[w]e need, in fact, only observe the course of events during and after the California gold discoveries to satisfy ourselves that these discoveries were responsible for a great deal more than a change in the significance of the unit in which values are expressed. Nor have we any difficulty in realizing – as did A. Smith – that the development of an efficient banking system may make a lot of difference to the development of a country's wealth." Kindleberger (1993) as well as other economic historians - for example Gershenkron (1962) - have ascribed primary importance to monetary matters when discussing economic growth episodes in Europe. On the other hand, in the mainstream macroeconomics the prevalent idea is that impact of monetary variables, including the international monetary system on the systematic wealth creation and the long run economic growth is low or none. Proponents of both neo-classical and endogenous growth theory do not see the monetary affairs as one of the factors affecting long-run growth rates.

The results of Baxter and Stockman (1989) and Flood and Rose (1985) indicate that there are very few differences in behavior of macroeconomic aggregates under different exchange rate regimes.

These results are challenged by work of Reinhart and Rogoff (2003). Reinhart and Rogoff (2003) point to an important observation that the behavior of inflation rate and income growth per capita depends on whether a unified or a dual (multiple) exchange rate arrangement prevails. For example, under unified exchange rate arrangements the average inflation is considerably lower than under dual (multiple) exchange rate arrangements. It seems that the pure existence of dual or multiple exchange rates have negative consequence on domestic inflation, or in other words the circumstances which lead to emergence of dual or multiple exchange rates have typically unfavorable influence on macroeconomic performance. The difference, while smaller, is also seen when growth of real per capita income is compared across countries. Specifically, for the period 1970-2001 Reinhart and Rogoff (2003, p. 39) show that in their large sample of countries the average annual inflation rate under unified exchange rate regime is 19.8%, while under dual or multiple exchange rate annual inflation rate is above 160%. Similarly average per capita GDP growth is higher (1.8%) under unified rate than under dual rate (0.8%).

Reinhard and Rogoff (2003) results point to second important conclusion. It is typically believed that inflation rate is substantially smaller under peg than under free float. However, Reinhard and Rogoff (2003) show that actually free float brings lower inflation than the peg, since it is the freely falling exchange rate regime where most of the inflation is created. In their data for the period 1970 till 2001 taking IMF official classification as given they obtain that average annual inflation rate under peg was 38.8% while under float it was 173.9%,. Actually the lowest inflation was under limited flexibility regimes 5.3% and even under managed float the inflation was higher than under peg (74.8 or 38.8% respectively). However, if classification of Reinhard and Rogoff (2003) is used than the highest inflation is under freely falling regime (4433.3%), the lowest under free float (9.4%), while under peg it is 15.9%, under limited flexibility 10.1% and under managed float 16.5%.

Reinhard and Rogoff (2003) also compare their classification to IMF official classification in terms of growth performance across exchange rate arrangements. Under de jure classification growth performance is weakest under free float (0.5% average annual per capita GDP growth) and highest under limited flexibility regimes (2.2%), under managed float (1.9%), while it equals 1.4% under the peg. However, Reinhard and Rogoff (2003) classification show the worst growth performance (-2.5%) under freely falling regime. Best performance is achieved under limited flexibility (2.4%), then free float (2.3%), peg (1.9%) and managed float (1.6%) follow, respectively.

Reinhart and Rogoff (2003, p.22) also show that for the developing countries the pre- and post-1973 behavior of de facto exchange rates are similar, when considering also the parallel market premia. This contradicts the prevailing belief that the pre-1973 regime was characterized by stability while the post-1973 regime by volatility.

Broda (2002) points to an important link between exchange rate regime and price level which seems significant for low and medium income countries. He shows that the national price levels of countries with similar level of development are strikingly different and that this difference cannot be fully explained by the Ricardo-Balassa-Samuelson hypothesis and neither by the Kravis-Lipsey-Bhagwati hypothesis which both suggest a positive relationship between the level of income and the price level. Ricardo-Balassa-Samuelson hypothesis suggests that the more developed is the country the higher is the price level because of the difference in productivity between tradables and non-tradables, while Kravis-Lipsey-Bhagwati hypothesis sees link between development and the price level through an argument that poorer countries labor intensity of non-tradables is higher than in richer countries. Broda (2002) provides an explanation building on the insights of Obstfeld and Rogoff (2000) and Corsetti and Pesenti (2001) that the price setting behavior of agents depends to a certain extent on the response of monetary authorities to real shocks. The intuition is that "in countries with no exchange rate flexibility, the monetary authority is unable to accommodate productivity and world preference shocks to avoid employment variation." Broda (2002, p. 2). Under sticky wages and fixed exchange rate regimes labor requires a wage premium (relative to labor under float) to be compensated for the larger employment variations.

Calvo and Mishkin (2003) put an emphasis to economic institutions especially those which help to promote fiscal and financial stability and those which help to build credibility of monetary institutions. They see these institutions as the most important factors explaining macroeconomic performance. Also they see deep connections between institutions and exchange rate regimes and 'this interdependence between institutions and exchange rate regimes help to explain the general empirical finding that whether a country has a fixed or flexible exchange rate tells us little about whether it has higher economic growth or smaller output fluctuations." Calvo and Mishkin (2003, p. 16).

It seems that there are costs and benefits associated with any type of exchange rate regime. Generally, there are no simple answers to the question whether to prefer fully flexible, intermediate or very rigid exchange rate regimes. It seems that the optimal regime may vary from case to case and from country to country. This seems to be the prevalent opinion in the literature; see for example Frankel (1999), Willamson (2000) and Gylfason (2002). Calvo and Mishkin (2003) are of the opinion that especially for the emerging economies there is not a one exchange rate regime which will always fit all the countries. "Instead, an informed choice of exchange rate regime requires a deep understanding of a country's economy, institutions, and political culture." (p.28).

Chapter 3

EXCHANGE RATE POLICY IN THE CENTRAL EUROPEAN COUNTRIES

This chapter deals with exchange rate relations of four former socialist countries, which had joined the European Union on 1st May 2004. These countries are the Czech Republic, Hungary, Poland, and the Slovak Republic with overall population around 65 million. The Czech and Slovak korunas are new on the world map of currencies since they emerged as legal tenders after the break-up of the former Czechoslovakia in 1993. The Polish zloty and Hungarian forint were currencies already in use during the socialist period.

These countries began the transformation process from very similar starting positions, at least to the extent that they all were former socialist countries which launched transition in 1989 or at the early 1990s. Also during the period 1990-2004 these countries face similar challenges: privatization, stabilization, liberalization, institution building, and general introduction of the market economy and democratic political structure. Furthermore, these countries have also very similar objectives, they all are eventually to introduce euro.

After the turbulence at the beginning of the 1990s it was a principal task for the monetary authorities of these countries to guarantee that their currencies were stable in domestic and international value. As this section shows this task was accomplished and today both korunas, zloty and forint represent stable currencies in both domestic as well as international context. In the near future, most probably till 2010, all these currencies are going to be replaced by the euro.

INITIAL STABILIZATION

These four countries had entered the transition process with significant monetary overhang, the extent of which differed across countries. Stabilization programs were introduced in order to prevent that excess money demand together with price and trade liberalization in the temporary falling income context transform into high inflation. Since income policies were considered controversial it was the monetary and exchange rate policies which took the lead at the stabilization process. These stabilization packages were to a certain extent similar to stabilization packages used for example in high inflation Latin America countries in the 1980s, even if at the beginning of transition in these countries – with Poland as exception - visible inflation was relatively low, however it was feared that price liberalization would generate significant inflation. Removal of state subsidies and above all pressures from relative price changes implied an environment in which it might be problematic to sell to the general public a temporary increase in price level as non-inflationary.

In the long run higher inflation has always money growth as a proximate cause, but the potential inflation at the beginning of the 1990s has at its origin a large shock stemming from the change in the social regime. As Blanchard et. all (1991) clarify this regime change has different impact on economic agents and may lead to inconsistent claims to income distribution. These claims could potentially generate inflation through monetizing budget deficits and/or through government accommodative wage policy aiming at preventing negative effects on labor. This was the case especially in countries which belonged to the former Soviet Union. However, the four Central European countries to a large extent have avoided such traps, but even in these countries it took approximately ten years to push inflation under ten percent per annum.

Under the socialist regime a large variety of exchange rates was used in practice of socialist planning besides the officially determined exchange rate. Consequently, one of the symbols of successful exchange rate policy is seen in the elimination of dual and multiple exchange rates in the first years of the transition. Already at the beginning of the 1990s one currency rate was introduced, i.e. the difference between the 'official' and parallel market rate had disappeared in these countries.

At the beginning of transition these countries had opted for such a level of their domestic currencies, which indicated large difference between the purchasing power parity and the actual nominal exchange rate, i.e. significant undervaluation relative to purchasing power has happened. Establishing a unified exchange rate involved a substantial devaluation. This initial devaluation depended on the intensity of inherited macroeconomic imbalances, and in particular on the extent of excess domestic demand inherited from the socialist past rather than on budget deficits and wage increases which were quite non-excessive at the first period of stabilization. Oblath (1994) argues that the extent of the initial devaluation depended on the extent of how far were these economies from the open foreign trade regime, i.e. other factors being equal, the further was the economy from an open trade regime and the more swift and radical was the trade liberalization, the larger was the necessary initial devaluation.

The need to stabilize was not controversial, however it was not obvious which stabilization strategy should be adopted. Among options were the orthodox stabilization policy involving fiscal and monetary policies and the heterodox policy including also income policies. Another option was between money-based stabilizations and exchange rate-based stabilization. We observe the predominance of exchange rate-based orthodox stabilizations. In the next chapter we provide a rather detailed analysis of the exchange-rate based stabilization program introduced in the Czech Republic in the early 1990s.

General Overview of the Macroeconomic Situation: 1990-2004

Generally, one needs to say that performance of these economies with respect to growth, inflation and exchange rate stability was impressive. The transformation of these economies from former socialist economies to the new European Union member countries has been successful.

Inflation performance in these countries is impressive. Despite high inflation in the early period of transition central bank policy pushed inflation to low levels. This effort was helped by low inflation in the western European countries, the most important trading partners, and thus imported inflation was rather unimportant. Credible monetary and exchange rate policy helped to decrease uncertainties concerning the future development and assisted in creating dis-inflationary expectations. Also the downward trend in consumer price inflation was helped by gradual exchange rate appreciation. Low inflation also reflected gradual weakening of the underlying political and social conflicts in these countries.

In 1993 no country in our sample had inflation lower than 20% per annum. This was already a progress since in 1991 – when in most countries the macroeconomic stabilization programs were initiated – the lowest inflation was 35%, in Hungary. In 2000 the highest inflation was in Slovakia with 12%, while Hungary and Poland had inflation around 10% while the Czech inflation was down to approximately 4 percent. This process continued also in the period 2003-2004 when annual average percentage change over preceding year went down to 4-6 percent as maximum; United Nations Economic Commission for Europe, various issues of Economic Survey of Europe.

All four countries developed modern tax system: value added tax and personal income tax were the key instruments of this new development. These countries encounter problems with unstable fiscal policy which increases their overall debt. At the beginning of the 1990s there was a relative tranquil period during which public debt was stagnant or declined. In the second half of the 1990s debt burdens began to rise. In overall the debt stock has risen during the transition period. As compared to emerging countries as a whole it seems that the situation in these new EU member economies is relatively consolidated.

Currently the most troublesome situation seems to emerge due to rising costs of pension and health care. Budget deficit are likely to remain until the pension and health care reforms are completed. Furthermore, the high costs of bank restructuring (covering losses of non-performing bank loans) are also responsible for the rise in the fiscal deficits especially in both countries of the former Czechoslovakia. There are also structural factors behind the widening fiscal imbalance as the size of government. Additional factor contributing to worsening of fiscal positions is increased spending as a result of election considerations. For example, in 2001 before the election the incumbent Hungarian government initiated public infrastructure programs and pledged to increase public sector wages. Furthermore the newly elected government initiated an even larger pay rise for the public sector. Similarly, the Czech Republic initiated a large-scale two-year fiscal stimulus program in 2001. Furthermore, there are problems on the revenue side, too, as the high tax burden – especially in Hungary - with incentives to avoid taxes.

Czech Republic has traditionally been a low-debt country and also its current debt indicators are favorable in relative terms. Slovakia is moderately indebted with higher both debt/export and debt/income ratio than the Czech Republic, but both these ratios appear to be stable and are not excessive. The nominal debt of Hungary is growing, and the country remains moderately indebted. In the first half of the 1990s Poland debt was partially restructured. Poland's debt grew in the second half of the 1990s, but today still the debt/GDP ratio is low. However, since Poland is a large economy thus less open, its debt/export ratio is very large.

In most years of transition the current account of these countries was characterized with deficit. The current account deficit is founded on the huge merchandise trade deficit, which is lowered by receipts from services. Significant current account deficits are financed for the most part by capital inflows.

The process of increased integration of these economies with the Western Europe is well reflected in the share of the European Union countries in their exports and imports. 'Westernization' of the former socialist countries is seen in the increasing share of developed economies in their total merchandise exports. In the early 1990s these were around 50% and in 2002 the share is getting close to 75%. On the other hand, the importance of the developing world is decreasing from approximately 12% to around 6% respectively; Fidrmuc, Horvath, Fidrmuc (2002).

In the first half of the 1990s the flow of foreign direct investment was an important factor only for small number of countries as Hungary, the Czech Republic and to a smaller extent Poland and the Slovak Republic. In the second half of the 1990s the picture is changing somewhat. The volume of inflows is still substantial in the Czech Republic, Hungary, but also in Slovakia, and Poland. The importance of foreign direct investment into Slovakia is rising in the recent years.

The most important issue which shadows the successful picture of transformation of these economies is the pertaining income gap between these countries and the more developed parts of Western Europe. For example, OECD (2004) documents that the gap in terms of purchasing power parity at 1995 prices is largest for Poland as compared to the OECD average. In 2003 at purchasing power parity Poland per capita income was \$ 10 460, while in the Slovak Republic \$ 10 933, Hungary \$12 389, the Czech Republic \$ 13 971, and average of the OECD was \$23 254. OECD (2004, p. 82). According to OECD (2004) the potential for faster future growth in these countries lies in introducing policies of higher labor utilization. So far the growth has been driven rather by labor productivity growth than by high labor utilization. OECD (2004, p. 83) reports that 'present levels of underemployment suggest that strong employment disincentives prevail in the tax and benefits system." Employment rates in these countries are very low, below 60% for Slovak Republic, Poland and Hungary, while in Switzerland are around 85%. This low employment rate is partially due to high out-of-work benefits. OECD (2004, p. 94) advices that decreasing labor related taxes, as well as easing employment protection and reducing out-of-work benefits would make important contributions to the growth pattern in these countries.

Exchange Rates and Exchange Rate Regimes in the Period 1990-2004

All four Visegrad countries began stabilization programs with fixed exchange rate regimes. Poland and the former Czechoslovakia introduced rigid pegs in January 1990 and January 1991, respectively. Hungary adopted an adjustable peg in March 1990. The choice of fixed exchange-rate regimes (in contrast to floating rates chosen by most Balkan and former Soviet Union countries) reflected the Visegrad countries' commitment to price stability. In addition, the Visegrad countries had sufficient foreign exchange reserves needed to sustain a fixed exchange rate. With time, all four countries significantly relaxed and eventually abandoned fixed exchange rates in favor of more flexible regimes. Nevertheless, the fixed exchange-rate regime at the beginning of transition was crucial for preventing run-away inflation, delivering macroeconomic stability, and introduction of current account convertibility. In order to ensure the credibility and sustainability of the peg, the currency had to undergo a substantial initial devaluation at the outset of transition. The devaluation also served to improve the competitiveness of domestic producers in the wake of foreign-trade liberalization.

The first step towards floating occurred in the second half of the 1990's when the Czech Republic, Poland, and Slovakia were pressured to extend their fluctuation bands. This step was in fact precipitated by the appreciation tendency of their currencies. However, the Czech Republic found itself facing a reversal of capital flows and a simultaneous decline of foreign direct investments, leading to the currency crisis of May 1997. As a result, the Czech Republic floated its currency rate as of May 27, 1997. A similar development unfolded in Slovakia, where a floating exchange rate has been adopted as of October 1, 1998, shortly after the September 1998 election. In January 1999, Poland switched to inflation targeting extended the fluctuation bands for Polish zloty to ±15%. Simultaneously, the National Bank of Poland announced a plan to float the Zloty. This step was eventually adopted by April 12, 2000. Hungary sustained a fixed exchange-rate regime (crawling peg with narrow fluctuation bands) until Spring 2001. On May 4, 2001, Hungary extended fluctuation bands from ±2.25 % to ±15%. Subsequently, Hungary followed Poland and introduced inflation targeting on June 12, 2001 and lifted the remaining foreign exchange restrictions as of June 15, 2001. It is often argued that the main reason behind the recent adoption of floating has been the liberalization of the capital account transactions.

This movement toward more flexible exchange rate arrangements necessitated due to untenable pressures for appreciation of the real exchange rate. Another reason for moving towards more flexible exchange rate regimes was that such arrangement could serve as better protection against potential speculative attacks. The Czech experience from May 1997 and the Russian experience from one year later was the local basis for such fears. However, Szapary (2001) makes an argument that Poland was not protected from the speculative attack and the sudden shift of market sentiments even after April 2000 when a move towards full float has occurred.

After an excessive devaluation at the beginning of the 1990s the restrictive policies of central banks helped to stabilize currencies. We notice a tendency for increased stability of these currencies, especially for the most stable currency in the region, the Czech koruna which currently (2004 fall) trades in comparison to the U.S. dollar for approximately the same value as in 1991, when for example forint value decreased to a half as compared to the dollar for the same period.

Despite the adoption of floating exchange rate regimes monetary authorities in these countries continue to view exchange rate stability as one of the major objectives of monetary policy. Therefore, monetary authorities frequently engage in interventions against fluctuations of the exchange rate (though not against trend development of the exchange rate). Hausmann, Panizza and Stein (2001) suggest that countries which have no pre-determined vision concerning the level of their exchange rate when they move towards flexible exchange rate arrangement do not need a large amount of international reserves to manage their currency. On the other hand, countries which introduce a floating exchange rate but have certain vision about the proper level of their currency keep a large cushion of international reserves. These authors then calculate the ratio of international reserves to the level of money supply (M2) and compare these data across emerging and developed countries for the period 1998 and 1999. For example, this ratio equaled to 0.33 for the Czech Republic, 0.43 for Poland 0.43, and 0.25 for Slovakia when G-3 average was much lower, i.e. 0.06. In these two years the Czech Republic and Slovakia have already moved towards a managed float with no official pre-announced exchange rate path, while in Poland crawling peg was still in use. These results would suggest that – among other factors - central bankers in these countries have quite clear vision about the proper level of their currency as compared the G-3 countries.

Another way at looking at this issue is that countries introducing inflation targeting also keep substantial international reserves when their exchange rate regime is either managed float or full float. Calvo and Mishkin (2003, p. 22) write that especially emerging market countries need to be concerned about the possibility of a run on their currency, and in addition a high pass-through coefficient could transfer weakening of domestic currency into straight inflation.

We understand it as a sign of maturity in the conduct of exchange rate policy that in our four countries from 2001 there was no substantial change in exchange rate regime. Quite to opposite, the stability of these currencies is magnified by the fact that some of these currencies significantly appreciated. Significant inflow of capital also acts towards pushing up the value of these currencies. In addition there is an upward pressure due to the Ricardo-Harrod-Balassa-Samuelson effect.

When evaluating the exchange rate regimes of the four new EU member countries in the period 1990-2004 we encounter as a general tendency: a move of the de jure exchange rate regimes towards more flexible options. In 1991 all four countries used hard peg arrangements, while in May 2004 Poland was on free float, the Czech Republic and Slovakia on managed float while Hungary had a target zone with wide borders resembling ERM 2 shadowing.

It seems also that inconsistencies between the de jure and de facto exchange rate regimes are on the decline. Levy-Yeyati and Sturzenegger (2003) classify the Czech Republic in 1995 as a dirty float when hard peg prevailed, in 1996 they classify dirty float/crawling peg when target zone with wide band was introduced. From 1997 till 2000 they classify the Czech exchange rate regime as a float. Levy-Yeyati and Sturzenegger classification is based on yearly data thus in those years where the exchange rate regime was changed their classification reflects a combination of both regimes. For example, the Czech Republic is classified as a float for 1997, when managed float was introduced only in May of 1997. Furthermore, Levy-Yeyati and Sturzenegger (2003) classify Poland from 1991 till 2000 as having a floating regime when in this period variety of de jure regimes prevailed, however from 2000 on Poland uses a fully flexible arrangement. Nerlich (2002) also points to the fact that in the last couple of years, especially after 2000, we observe that the de facto regimes are getting closer to the de jure regimes, "which might indicate a continuously higher credibility of the institutions and capacity building in the accession countries." Nerlich (2002, pp.14-15). Nehrlich (2002) also raises a valid point that while there were shifts in the exchange rate regimes "these shifts were, with a few exceptions, not related to currency crises but the result of proactive policy management, which was largely facilitated by the institutional framework for EU integration." Nehrlich (2002, p. 3).

Nehrlich (2002) divides the development of exchange rate regimes in these countries into three period: the stabilization phase 1990-1994 when in all four countries fixed exchange rate regime prevailed; the transition period where in all countries except Hungary movement from intermediate towards flexible regime occurs: in Slovakia since 1998, in the Czech Republic since 1997 and in Poland since 2000; and the preparatory phase pre euro introduction period in which in three Slavic countries float prevails while in Hungary intermediate exchange rate arrangement prevails.

Building credible monetary institutions was a difficult task however one can say that in all four new EU member countries this task was accomplished. Today, central banks in these countries to a large extent perform a very credible policy, i.e. their commitment to price and currency stability is credible. This creates hopefully a good pre-requisite for efforts which will conclude by introduction of the euro in these countries.

Euro and the New Central European Member Countries

Economic and Monetary Union (EMU) is a union in which a single currency is used in those EU countries which joined the EMU. In the EMU all exchange rate controls are abolished and there is a free movement of capital. Exchange rates are irrevocably fixed and a European Central Bank is in charge of a common monetary policy.

EMU had evolved in the 1990s. In the first (preparatory) stage – between 1990 and December 1993 – completion of the internal market was achieved, which involved free movement of people, goods, services and capital. In this stage also co-ordination of macroeconomic policies between the member states included attempts to exchange rate stability. In the second stage the European Monetary Institute was established which was replaced by the European Central Bank in 1998. In the final stage from January 1 1999 Economic and Monetary Union emerged with irrevocably fixed values of national currencies towards the euro, finally, from January 2002 the euro emerged also in everyday life of the eurozone countries.

An argument that a given territory requires a fixed exchange rate to reap benefits from internal markets is controversial, but nevertheless popular. Arguments were typically used that countries could not reap full gains from the internal market unless exchange rate risk is eliminated. However, three EU member countries had opted not to introduce the euro. Two of them, Denmark and the United Kingdom negotiated opt-out clauses, while Sweden is simply postponing the entry into the union. Gylfason (2002) writes that these countries fear that adoption of the euro may prevent them to achieve full employment at home. "The countries have a history – a pretty successful record, some would say, albeit not consistently so – of devaluing or floating their currencies to keep domestic unemployment under control. ... The difference of opinion in this case thus centers on the question of which should come first: labor market liberalization or monetary union. The Swedes are not, at least not yet, confident that the structure and functioning of the Swedish economy, and of the Swedish labor market in particular, is flexible enough to adopt to the adoption of the euro." Gylfason (2002, p.4).

As far as the membership of our four new EU member countries in the EMU is concerned the economic analysis is not the only criterion one should attach importance to. The European integration project, the European Union, as well as the Economic and Monetary Union is as much political project as it is an economic one. Membership in the monetary union has its political value, and while there is some political opposition towards membership in the EU, it seems there is little political opposition – after entering the EU – against entering the EMU. It is important to note that we have no signs that the new EU member countries would like to avoid joining the eurozone as it happens in some western countries. As Szapary (2001) claims, "these accession countries, with their small, open economies, have a strong interest in joining the euro zone, which will offer them a number of economic advantages, including lower risk premiums, interest rates, and transaction costs."

Before joining the European Union the accession countries were to fulfill membership requirements. These represented a broad set of requirements, as summarized in the Copenhagen criteria, which consisted of assurances concerning democracy and human rights as well as of fully functioning market economy. European Commission was annually assessing the progress of the accession countries in meeting these criteria. Today, it seems to be an accepted view that countries, which joined the European Union in May 2004 have fulfilled the Copenhagen political criteria. These countries are still expected – among other issues - to improve bankruptcy proceedings, augment protection of intellectual property rights, and tackle the corruption.

The EU accession process does not set specific requirements for fiscal and monetary policies, although sustainability of macroeconomic policies is a central part of the determination of whether the accession country is ready or not for the entry. However, macroeconomic requirements are precisely defined when it comes to entry into the euro area. The EU has decided that for the new EU members there will be no opt-out clause, i.e. they all need to join the eurozone after they fulfill the entry requirements. .

In theory, the accession to EMU could take place at the earliest in 2006, that is, after two years of participation in ERM-2 when the new member joins ERM-2 immediately after EU accession (there is no requirement to do so, and none of the countries did so). The optimal time to enter EMU may differ for countries, and this is probably one explanation of why there are different visions concerning the joining of the EMU, but it is expected that all join the EMU till 2010. Currently (Spring 2005) expectation grows that Hungary will join the EMU later.

It seems that the parallel current account and fiscal deficit may require some adjustment periods for at least some of the applicants before they are able to meet the Maastricht criteria. Maastricht criteria were introduced to guarantee that all member countries impose fiscal prudence and thus free-riding as well as attempts to seek bail-outs from the European Central Bank can be ruled out. The new member countries will join the Economic and Monetary Union with derogation till they comply with the Maastrich convergence criteria.

Criteria for the EMU membership are the following:

- exchange rate stability: two-year membership in the Exchange Rate Mechanism and ensure that the exchange rate is stable before euro adoption; the aim is to prevent competitive devaluation before entering the eurozone;
- inflation: to keep the inflation rate inside the 1.5% point above the average of the three best-performing EU member countries over the latest twelve months before joining the eurozone. Question most often asked in this respect is whether an 'inflation premium' resulting from fast real economic growth due to the convergence process and the Ricardo-Harrod-Balassa-Samuelson effect will be accounted in some way by the European authorities. Under the assumption that the real convergence between the old and new EU members would occur then higher productivity growth in new member countries will lead to higher inflation rates in these countries, which might lead to real exchange rate appreciation "Under these conditions countries that pursue a fixed rate strategy in the run-up to the introduction of the euro might encounter difficulties fulfilling the inflation convergence criterion. Thus, there have been a number of suggestions to take these effects into account when assessing the adherence to the inflation criterion. .... It appears, however, that such proposals will not be acceptable." Hochreiter (2001, p.7). Hochreiter (2001) raises another interesting question that what would be the procedure if the set of three lowest inflation countries would include countries remaining outside the eurozone.
- long-term interest rate: should stay within 2%-points of the average three best-performing countries. It is thought that if the inflation criterion is satisfied the interest rate criterion will be most likely satisfied, too.
- fiscal criteria: public deficit below 3% of GDP and public debt below 60% of GDP. This is probably the most challenging criteria for the new member countries. After joining the EU the member countries are subject to this criterion even if penalties are in place only after joining the eurozone. Coricelli and Ercolani (2002) quoting Buiter and Grafe (2002) write that the rationale for the 3% deficit ceiling derives from the ratio of public investment to GDP of the member of the European Union during the period of 1960-1990. The strongest argument against this ceiling may be that it does not take into consideration the cyclical property of the economy, as Coricelli and Ercolani (2002, p. 16) write "it does not exert sufficient pressure for adjustment during good times." However, these criteria were designed with the intention to minimize inflationary pressures in the euro zone and thus to avoid free ride behavior of less responsible governments which would benefit from importing low inflation and low interest rates but would not launch sound fiscal policy. Coricelli and Ercolani (2002) make an argument in favor of more flexible fiscal rules. They argue that for new member countries it would be difficult to obey by the fiscal rules due to higher volatility of output and larger expenditures to public sphere. They write that "without changing existing rules in the European Union, it is likely that candidate countries will have to undertake costly and inefficient adjustments at the last minute that will prove very costly and inefficient for their economies." Coricelli and Ercolani (2002, p. 2). Similar argument about the last minute changes is raised by Szapary (2001), who argues that because of the Balassa-Samuelson effect the Maastricht inflation criteria can be achieved through restrictive monetary and fiscal policies, which may jeopardize growth or through appreciation of the nominal value

of the currency which has negative effect on the competitiveness. "The candidate country will maintain very tight monetary policy and resort to various techniques (for example, freezing administered prices or lowering consumption taxes) to squeeze down inflation prior to accession, only to shift gears after it enters EMU." Szapary (2001, p.4).

As have been already argued there is some controversy concerning the application of the Maastricht criteria to the new member countries. The controversy lies in the fact that too strict an interpretation of the Maastricht criteria could be counterproductive. Some authors as Andreff (1999) argue that catch-up requirements counteract the nominal convergence requirements. This is not the opinion of the representative of the Eurosystem, for example Padoa-Schioppa (2000) writes that "*nominal* convergence, understood as progress towards the nominal Maastricht criteria over the medium term, and *real* convergence, understood as the process of real income catching up with levels in the EU and the euro area, do *not* conflict and should be pursued in parallel." (p.1. italics in the original). Also Havrylyshyn, Izvorski and van Rooden (1998) argue that these conditions, especially reduced public expenditures, are the key for sustainable growth prospects.

Real convergence per se is irrelevant for the adoption of euro in the new EU member countries. If this would be otherwise one could expect a very long process of euro adoption. Such proposals, while they had appeared were later refuted. "Proposals to link the adoption of the euro to some minimum per capita GDP benchmark thus amount to the request of a sizeable postponement of its adoption. It seems that the discussion more recently has moved away from such regressive propositions." Hochreiter (2001, p.6). In a slightly different context Szapary (2001, p.5) proposes to tie the Maastricht inflation criteria to the per capita income. "The reference for high-income countries would be the average inflation rate in the highest per capita income group, and the reference for the low-income countries would be the average inflation rate in the lowest per capita income group."

One can raise an issue whether the accession countries would be able to meet the fiscal targets required for the EMU accession. Public debt levels do not appear to be a major obstacle at this stage. To consolidate the fiscal situation may get exceedingly difficult after joining the EU since the membership itself leads to new claims on public spending. For example, while it is expected that the new member countries will be recipients of structural funds, in order to absorb them they will have to provide matching national funds, which represent a net new claim on government budgets especially in environmental protection and infrastructure.

Joining the Eurozone is a necessity for the new member countries, since no opt-out clause is available for them. This process is most likely to happen in three distinguished periods.

1. In the pre-EU accession period variety of exchange rate regimes are possible however this phase had ended on 1st May 2004. In this period the four Central European countries opted initially for fixed exchange rate regimes, and later moved towards more flexible regimes. From early stabilization towards EU accession no preferred exchange rate strategy is prescribed by the European Union.
2. In the post-EU accession period the new member countries are sooner or later expected to join the ERM2 mechanism, were the domestic currency has a parity fixed to the euro. The ERM 2 membership is for minimum of two years. In this period

countries become to gain the status of 'countries with a derogation" as they are on the way to adopt the euro and thus their exchange rate regime needs to be compatible with what is vaguely defined as the 'common interest' of the eurozone member countries. This may happen either in a target zone regime with ± 15% band or in other regime considered compatible with the ERM 2 since there is no clear exchange rate regime requirement. Padoa-Schioppa (2000, p.1) relating to the plurality of approaches in the choice of exchange rate regimes writes that "the Eurosystem believes that a variety of approaches should be feasible without compromising equality of treatment." In the run-up period to EU and EMU membership there is no appropriate exchange rate regime. The task for the monetary authorities is to ensure external and internal macroeconomic stability, which could be guaranteed by different policy mix. The most important fact is that these governments were at least to a certain extent able to reject populist pressure and showed strong political commitment to both internal and external stability.

3. In the third period the domestic currency is irrevocably fixed to euro and euro is introduced as a legal tender.

The European authorities as Padoa-Schioppa (2000) writes consider this three step process analogous to steps done by those countries which had joined the EU earlier: first the European Community was established then the European Monetary System and eventually some of EU member countries adopted the euro.

Currencies in these countries are on the real exchange rate appreciation trend that is one of the reason these countries are not in hurry to lock their nominal variables to nominal Maastricht targets. This real appreciation trend materializes either in real exchange rate appreciation if the nominal exchange rate is fixed or in nominal exchange rate appreciation for countries with more flexible exchange rate arrangements. Today, early Winter 2005 none of the countries had joined the ERM 2, and it is typically expected that the Central European countries will join the eurozone at the earliest at 2008-2009. Kocenda (2004) expects all four countries to join the eurozone at 2010 at the latest.

At the beginning of the transition process dollar had played – to a certain extent – the anchor role (peg towards dollar, important role of dollar in currency baskets), as the time passed the euro had considerable increased its role as a reference currency for these countries. Euro's importance compared to the dollar had increased mainly due to increased trade linkages between these countries and the member countries of the eurozone and other EU countries. This role is furthermore strengthened by the ownership structure in domestic banks, since large section of domestic bank assets in accession countries are controlled by eurozone commercial banks. Today, already the euro represents an (indirect) nominal anchor for all of the new member countries.

Exchange rate risks remain still high especially in countries with high fiscal deficit and rising debt. Volatility of short-term capital flows and possible currency crisis before joining the EMU structures is still a possibility.

Any country can adopt the euro unilaterally, i.e. without the consent of the European Central Bank as the legal tender. That can be done either by introducing euro as a sole legal tender but also as a parallel legal tender. Dornbusch and Giavazzi (1998) had already proposed for the four Central European countries to give up their monetary sovereignty. Dornbusch and Giavazzi proposed currency boards as a possible solution arguing that currency board offers completely credible system to protect from currency risks. Later Rostowski (2001a, 2001b) and Wojczik (2000) discussed the issue of unilateral euroization for the Central European countries, especially for Poland. This discussion on the possibility of unilateral euroization has an interesting political dimension since the official position of the European Community is not in support of the unilateral euroization while it supports other very rigid exchange rate regimes as the currency board system in the ERM 2 mechanism. Padoa-Schioppa (2000, p.8) writes: "We in the Eurosystem, however, have taken a strong view that 'intermediate' regimes have their justification. ... In this trajectory, if we want the exchange rate to be adjustable when required and, at the same time, to play an anchoring role, probably neither of the two corner solutions is optimal as a general rule. In fact, it may be preferable to have an exchange rate regime which plays a disciplinary role but is adjustable enough to accommodate the catching-up process. ERM II is precisely that." Also in a more official tone: "The Eurosystem has taken a position on currency boards and euroisation, as has the ECOFIN Council. Basically, the position is 'no' to euroisation and 'perhaps' to currency boards. What does this mean? Euroisation as such is considered inconsistent with the Treaty, and not feasible. ..... the appropriateness of currency boards would have to be determined on a case-by-case basis." Padoa-Schioppa(2000, p.9).

It seems then, that these countries will join the eurozone in a similar fashion as the current eurozone members did, and thus the official euroization is not an option.

Optimum Currency Area Criteria and the Euro Adoption

Goldberg (1999) argued that the optimum currency area considerations should not be taken into account when transition economies decide about their exchange rate regimes. She argues that supply elasticities needed for the exchange rate to be effective tool for stabilization are not present at the beginning of transition. "In such an economic environment, the traditional optimal stabilization policy criteria applied to output and/or balance of payments targets may not be relevant for the transition economy's decision about whether or not to implement or maintain an independent currency." (p.3) She argues further that "the traditional optimum currency area criteria, interpreted in terms of optimal real stabilization policy, are only useful if *the exchange rate is able to effectively perform the task of short-term stabilization (output or balance-of-payments) to which it is assigned.*"[italics in original] (p. 3) It seems that this argument was quite powerful at the beginning of transition, however it loses its validity in the pre-euro adoption discussions. Consequently, we observe – especially in the late 1990s – appearance of papers dealing with the issue of optimum currency areas in the context of transition European economies. Several studies discussed below consider the issue of the symmetry of shocks affecting transition economies.

Horvath (2000) measures the correlation of shocks across transition and current eurozone countries. His study presents results in support of the prevalence of idiosyncratic shocks between western EU members and the transition countries. Fidrmuc and Korhonen (2001) assert that the correlation of supply shocks differs greatly from country to country, although some accession countries are "at least as well correlated with the euro area shocks as are many current members of the monetary union." (p. 24). Frenkel and Nickel (2002) conclude that "there are still differences in the shocks and in the adjustment process to shocks between the euro area and the CEECs. However, several individual CEECs exhibit shocks and shock adjustment processes that are fairly similar to some euro area countries."

Table 2 below summarizes the empirical results of these studies.

Table 2. Shocks between EMU, Germany and Accession Countries

	Supply Shocks				Demand Shocks			
	Germany		EMU		Germany		EMU	
	A	B	C	A	A	B	C	A
Czech Republic	0.538	-0.05	0.04	0.052	0.321	0.10	-0.15	0.213
Poland	-0.494	0.00	0.08	-0.690	-0.200	0.14	0.28	0.217
Slovak Republic	0.384	-0.04	0.05	0.182	-0.097	0.04	-0.05	-0.433
Hungary	0.263	0.28	0.46	0.726	-0.197	-0.40	0.25	0.122

Correlation values based on structural vector autoregressive estimations.
A. Frenkel and Nickel (2002); quarterly data for the period 1993:1-2001:4.
B. Horvath (2000): quarterly data for the period 1993:1-2000:3. for Hungary 1995:1-2000:3.
C. Fidrmuc and Korhonen (2001)

Boone and Maurel (1999) using dynamic common factor analysis provides evidence for 'symmetry between the transition countries business cycle and that of Germany, and to a lower extent that of the EU." Boone and Maurel (1999, p.12). Babetski (2003) finds that an increase in trade intensity and a decrease in exchange rate volatility is associated with demand shock convergence, and he interprets his result as in support of the endogeneity of the optimum currency areas. Babetski, Boone and Maurel (2003) introduce time varying correlation measurements and thus they are able to differentiate between the overall transition period and the most recent period. Their results show an ongoing process of demand shock convergence and supply shock divergence.

These results may indicate that shocks among EMU accession and incumbent countries, in particular Germany tend to be uncorrelated. On one hand, these results may imply that proceeding with the union could be quite costly for the participants. On the other hand, they may simply highlight the importance of non-economic factors in creating viable currency unions; Horvath and Ratfai (2004).

Chapter 4

CASE STUDIES

CZECH EXCHANGE RATE REGIME: FROM EARLY SUCCESS TO CURRENCY CRISIS

This is a substantially abridged version of the working paper published with Jiri Jonas at the ZEI University of Bonn in 1998.

At the beginning of 1990 Czechoslovakia was at the start of a new experiment. Compared to Hungary and Poland, the reform socialist economies, the Czech Republic (Czechoslovakia) represented an anti-reform strand in the socialist movement in the 1970s and 1980s. This might suggest that compared to these two countries the Czech Republic was supposed to be in disadvantage at the beginning of the transition. However, the socialist reform process was not managed well, and even though it introduced some aspects of the market economy it began to be partially a liability when the transition process began. It left Hungary and Poland with high foreign indebtedness, medium to high level inflation, rising government debt, excessively powerful trade unions, etc. It seems that merits of reform socialism were in weakening the power structure, and not in promoting macroeconomic stability or potential for higher future real growth rates. Some aspects of socialist reform, as for example small scale private enterprises, which took many years for the reformers to introduce in the old regime quickly emerged in the first months and years of transition.

In the period from 1970 till 1989 in the Czech Republic consumer price index did not exceed on yearly basis a 3 percent growth, wages grew slower than the officially measured productivity, hard currency debt was comparatively low. Also monetary overhang at the Czech Republic was lower than in Poland or Hungary. For a more detailed description of the pre-transition macroeconomic situation see Bruno (1993), and Brada and Kutan (1997). Furthermore, the Czech economic policy makers could take advantage of the inherited authority of the Czech state, which had been practically unchallenged by non-state interests during the socialist period. Also relative weakness of some civil institutions such as labor unions, local governments, non-governmental organizations allowed to introduce market institutions in a relatively high speed.

Macroeconomic stability combined with the decisive pro-western and pro-market oriented economic policy and rhetoric has made the Czech transition the darling of international investors and commentators in the first half of the 1990s. Favorable assessments of the Czech experience abounded. Part of this success - at least as it was perceived - was also the Czech exchange rate policy. "... it is safe to say that the Czech Republic's approach [to the exchange rate management] was the most successful," was argued in CEPR/Institute for East West Studies Brief, No.2, November 1996, p.1. We take this quotation from Brada and Drabek (1998, p. 16). "Of all five East European countries, the Czechoslovak stabilization was virtually a textbook case - the initial price shock was followed by relative price stability." Bruno (1993, p.219).

A fixed exchange rate regime was introduced on January 1st 1991, and persisted for more than six years. It was seen by some policy makers and by part of the public as a symbol of the Czech success. However, a worsening of the macroeconomic situation in the second half of the 1990s, combined with political instability at the beginning of 1997 and with contagious effect from the Asian crisis led to the abandonment of the peg, and to the introduction of the managed float regime in May 1997. This has changed the perception of the Czech transition performance, and a more negative view emerged. See for example Buch and Heinrich (1997).

In the following we re-examine the Czech experience with the exchange rate regime(s). At the beginning of the Czech transition, the question of the type of the exchange rate regime to be chosen was among the most prominent ones. This was to be decided in an obvious discontinuity to the previous policy regime. The past could not provide a reliable benchmark, but it was also not clear where to look for advice. There were no ready-made solutions for the selection of the exchange rate regimes in transition economies. Furthermore, it was also not clear what should be the new level of the exchange rate. With the advantage of hindsight we review this process.

Optimal Currency Area Literature and the Czech Experience

It seems reasonable to assume that the working of a particular exchange rate regime will depend on the characteristics of the economy in which the regime works, and this is exactly what the optimum currency area literature intends to study. There are two established results in the optimum currency area literature. One is that a higher degree of flexibility of the exchange rate is most beneficial for countries experiencing different disturbances than their most important trading partners. The second result is in terms of economic openness: a country with high degree of mobility of factors of production should favor fixed exchange rate regime. This result is extended also to the openness in terms of market of goods and services; Guitián (1994, p. 19). We ask whether for the Czech Republic the applications of these two results, and also of some other criteria used in the optimum currency area literature, could lead to some decisive answer concerning the exchange rate regime.

First, we discuss the issue of the asymmetry of shocks. We ask whether the Czech Republic prior to the transition period, was exposed to asymmetric shocks compared to its Western European neighbors. We consider as 'neighbors' the Western European countries, since it was quite likely that if a peg was chosen, it would be a Western currency or a basket of Western currencies to which the koruna would be pegged. Intuition would suggest asymmetry, and thus also the adoption of flexible exchange rates to ease the cost of adjustment to these shocks. This intuition is supported by the results presented in table 3 below. In deriving the supply and demand shocks we followed the approach pioneered by Bayoumi and Eichengreen (1992) who propose a method of identification of supply and demand shocks in a structural vector autoregressive framework. They identify as real supply shocks those shocks which have permanent effect on real output, and as nominal demand shocks those which have only a temporary effect on real output.

We use yearly data on real output and real output deflator for the period 1950-1989.The source for Czechoslovak data is Mitchell (1992). Data for real and nominal GDP (GNP) for western countries are taken from the International Financial Statistics CD-ROM. The usefulness of these results is affected by the quality of data as well as by the effect of distorted prices and administrative regimes used in the socialist period, and by the fact that the asymmetry of the past does not need to follow in the future if there is a regime shift. For these reason we repeated the exercise using quarterly data for the period 1990-1997. What is probably a bit more surprising is that this asymmetry prevails also in this period. Compared to the Western European countries the Czech Republic was exposed to different types of shocks both in the socialist period as well as in the transition period. Again, the validity of these results could be challenged based on the quality of data. Also as Funke (1997) shows the quarterly estimation using this technique gives lower values also for correlations among western countries. To the extent to which we can infer from these results, it seems that the asymmetry of shocks would have probably required a flexible exchange rate arrangement.

Mundell (1961) argues that if asymmetric shocks prevail, the peg can still be a reasonable alternative if labor mobility is high. Countries with high labor mobility could opt for pegged exchange rates. Sufficiently high labor mobility within the country serves to lighten the effect of asymmetric shocks, since it allows workers from regions hit negatively to move to regions which were positively affected. Empirical studies dealing with labor mobility usually measure dispersion of unemployment rates across different regions and countries. Fidrmuc, Horvath and Fidrmuc (1999) using the data from 1992 for 76 Czech counties show that labor mobility have served to mitigate the effects of asymmetric shocks. However, the size of this effect is in fact very modest. Thus it seems that the labor mobility was not able to cope with asymmetry of shocks and this again supports the case for the flexible regime.

Kenen (1969) argues that for a well-diversified economy the importance of asymmetric shocks will be much smaller than for a less-diversified economy. In Table 4 below we present shares of different sectors in the total production for the Czech Republic, Germany and the US. This GDP structure in the Czech Republic is relatively similar to that of the most advanced market economies. The relatively well diversified character of the Czech economy could work towards decreasing the weight of asymmetric shocks.

The second established criterion in the optimum currency area literature concerns the degree of openness. The more open is an economy, the more it should be inclined to use fixed exchange rate arrangements. Data on openness presented in Table show that even under the socialist regime the country belonged to the more open European economies. This relatively high openness, comparable to countries as Austria or Denmark would be probably a strong argument for choosing a peg.

Table 3. Some Criteria of Optimum Currency Area Theory

	Correlation of Shocks				Openness
	1950-1989		1990-1997		
	Supply Shocks	Demand Shocks	Supply Shocks	Demand Shocks	1988
USA	-0.26	-0.18	-0.27	-0.01	11.2
Germany	-0.02	-0.01	-0.32	-0.12	53.9
United Kingdom	-0.14	-0.11	0.01	0.02	50.1
France	0.12	-0.13	0.12	0.23	42.6
Italy	0.19	0.30	0.24	-0.29	38.3
Austria	0.12	0.13	---	---	74.7
Switzerland	0.05	0.04	---	---	72.6
Netherlands	0.03	-0.04	---	---	105.1
Belgium	-0.12	0.15	---	---	141.9
Denmark	-0.05	0.06	0.12	-0.28	61.6
Spain	0.05	0.26	---	---	38.3
Portugal	-0.30	-0.07	---	---	78.4
Greece	0.15	0.06	---	---	54.5
Ireland	0.01	-0.20	---	---	115.1
Sweden	0.18	0.08	---	---	63.1
Norway	0.10	-0.03	---	---	74.0
Finland	0.00	0.20	---	---	49.5
Czechoslovakia	---	---	---	---	67.8
Czech Republic[1]	---	---	---	---	59.0
Czech Republic [2]	---	---	---	---	86.8

Based on yearly data for the period 1950-89, and quarterly data for 1990:1-97:4. The quarterly shocks calculated only for countries which had all data in the given period in the August 1998 IFS-CDROM. Openness calculated according to Summers and Heston (1991) data set as percentage share of exports plus imports in the nominal GDP. 1/ indicates openness in 1991. 2/ indicates openness in 1991 including the trade with Slovakia.

Table 4. GDP Structure: Czech Republic, United States, and Germany

	Czech Republic	USA	Germany
Agriculture	6.5	2.3	2.1
Manufacturing	26.7	22.2	38.3
Construction	5.2	5.5	6.1
Mining, Energy and Utilities	10.3	5.8	4.2
Services	51.3	64.2	49.4

Sources: Data for the United States and Germany are from Masson and Taylor (1992). Data for Czech Republic refer to 1993.

There are also some other criteria used in the optimal currency literature. One of them is the degree of financial market developments. At the beginning of the 1990s the Czech financial market was very thin and relatively underdeveloped. To choose a free float under such conditions could possible lead to a very volatile exchange rate. Another criterion is the degree of geographic concentration of trade. A high degree of concentration of trade with a large country would probably create an incentive to peg the domestic currency to that of the large country. If Western Europe is expected to be the largest trade partner, it would then indicate the usefulness of some kind of peg to the German mark. Fleming (1971) raised the importance of similarity of inflation rates between two countries which seems to facilitate the implementation of fixed exchange rate arrangements. If two countries peg their currencies but they exhibit very different inflation rates, then this is likely to generate a real exchange rate appreciation putting the balance-of-payment targets into jeopardy. At the beginning of transition process it was quite probable to expect that turbulent domestic developments, and possible social conflicts, would lead to higher domestic inflation than in the neighboring Western European countries. Thus, this criterion would suggest to opt for the flexible regime.

In this Section we considered the most important criteria suggested by the optimal currency area literature. These results point to some relevant considerations, but they do not have the operational precision needed in a decision making about the exchange rate regime. Our conclusion then cannot be completely definite. We cannot say that 'the theory of optimum currency areas proves that the Czech Republic should follow particular exchange rate regime'. This stresses the importance of the criteria discussed in the next Section.

Exchange Rate Regime and the Stabilization Program

From the onset of the transition, far-reaching price liberalization became one of the cornerstones of reform strategy. The main objective of the macroeconomic policy during this period was to prevent a rise in inflation in the aftermath of price liberalization, i.e., that an inevitable jump in price level does not affect nominal contracts in the economy and perpetuates the price increase. This is probably the main difference between the Czech and Latin American stabilization programs. While in the latter, the main task of the stabilization was to bring down persisting high inflation, in the former it was to prevent inflation from erupting. In the Czech situation there were no institutional arrangements as backward indexation of wages, so there was no need to forget the inflationary memory of the past, since there was almost none. Then the success of the anti-inflationary effort was more a function of the future expectations and the credibility of the government which had pursued it.

It was necessary to achieve that future nominal contracts be guided not by the present temporary price jump, but by other variable that would anchor the agents' expectations about inflation. This role of the nominal anchor could be assigned either to some monetary aggregate or to an exchange rate. Fischer (1986) has investigated this question. His analysis shows that exchange rate based stabilization is generally less costly than money based stabilization. In each case, income policy could be - and it was in the Czech case - used as additional element of the stabilization strategy. Under money based or exchange rate based stabilization programs the wage disturbances can be a serious problem. This was a reason why in 1990, a commission consisting of representative of government, trade union and managers agreed that in 1991 a nominal wage increase will not exceed 5 percent, if the inflation rate is not higher than 25 percent in the first quarter of 1991. Higher nominal wage increases were possible, but a decline of real wages by 12 percent had to be accepted in any case. Excess wages were taxed at a prohibitive rate. New private firms and ventures with foreign participation were exempted from these rules. Wage controls were maintained until July 1995. An attempt to abolish them at the beginning of 1993 had led to excessive wage increase, and to their re-introduction in July 1993.

A main requirement for successful stabilization based on a monetary nominal anchor is relative stability or predictable changes of demand for money. It was expected that the demand for money during the transition will become difficult to predict. Begg (1997, p. 39) presents results that indicate that among all transition countries velocity (ratio of broad money to the GDP) was the most stable in the Czech Republic. This does not of course mean that monetary targeting would be easy, since it always includes some forecast of real output and prices which was a considerably hazardous exercise in the early 1990s.

Under the circumstances when demand for money underwent large and frequent shifts which were difficult to predict with a reasonable degree of accuracy, there was a risk that the pursuit of a predetermined path of money growth could result in substantial shifts in monetary conditions, and that a given path of growth of some monetary aggregate would not be able to serve as an effective nominal anchor. In addition there was an attempt in 1990 to use money supply (the volume of banking credits) as a nominal anchor, but the experience was that it did not work satisfactorily enough; Hrncir (1993, p.8). The instability of the demand for money has also represented a particularly pressing problem at times of high and/or variable inflation that prevailed in some countries in transition at the start of price liberalization. Moreover, there was a widespread currency substitution of foreign for domestic currency. Under such circumstances, monetary aggregates are difficult to use to influence households' and firms' expectations about future growth of liquidity and prices, which could undermine the effectiveness of stabilization based on monetary aggregates.

Using the exchange rate as a nominal anchor instead has several advantages. First, in contrast to monetary aggregates, the exchange rate is transparent, highly visible and easier to understand to the broad public. At the start of the reform, both the government and the central bank did not have any record of policy making under the market system, and their credibility had to be first earned, and for this reason, it was desirable to base the stabilization program on a visible and easy-to-follow variable. A credible nominal exchange rate anchor can also affect inflation expectations, and thereby can increase the effectiveness of the stabilization strategy. At the beginning of the transition the past did not provide clear guide to price and wage setting, and expectations about the future have played a correspondingly more prominent role in this process. If economic agents are confident that the exchange rate anchor will produce price stability or at least low inflation in the future, and if these expectations affect wage and price negotiations, inflation could be reduced and prices stabilized relatively quickly. An additional argument for an exchange rate anchor comes from the experience of some inflationary countries where in the absence of another reliable measuring rod the pricing agents often use the exchange rate as an indicator to which they attach their decisions even if their product is not tradable. This is the so called "dentist effect." See Bruno (1993, p.222).

However, under certain circumstances, exchange rate-based stabilization can have negative impacts on the economy. One objection raised against pegging exchange rate is that at the initial stages of the reform, it is uncertain whether stabilization will succeed, and the fixed exchange rate need not be credible. See Blanchard et al. (1991). Maintaining a fixed exchange rate that is not credible could require high interest rates that could hurt growth. Another problem of a nominal exchange rate anchor is that after pegging the exchange rate, inflation in the domestic country would still remain higher than in the country to whose currency the domestic currency is pegged, with possible subsequent (potentially unsustainable) appreciation of a real exchange rate.

A third potential problem with pegging the exchange rate is the need to have a sufficient level of foreign reserves. By tying the value of its currency to another currency, a country commits itself to enter the market to maintain the established parity. This could be done by affecting the demand and/or supply of domestic currency relative to foreign currencies, either by directly selling or buying domestic currency, or by changing interest rates, thereby affecting relative attractiveness of domestic and foreign currency denominated assets. From a practical point of view, relying solely on interest rate policy is not feasible, and a country that maintains parity has to sell or buy its currency from time to time. To be able to do so, it needs to keep certain minimum amount of foreign reserves, or to have immediate access to credit lines. At the end of 1990, when the discussion about the exchange rate regime culminated, the Czech Republic's official reserves fell below US$ 1 billion, indeed a meager amount to use for exchange rate support. This could have been potentially a large obstacle to the introduction of a credible exchange rate peg.

Nevertheless, compared with the problems of the monetary-based stabilization, potential shortcomings of exchange rate-based stabilization strategy appeared in the end relatively less important, and the Czech Republic has opted for pegging the koruna vis-a-vis the basket of five currencies of countries that played an important role in its foreign trade, and which enjoyed domestic price stability. One factor that weighed in favor of introducing a fixed exchange rate was the financial assistance provided to the Czech Republic by the International Monetary Fund under the stand-by arrangement. During the discussion preceding the program, the Fund argued in favor of using a nominal exchange rate anchor, and having been aware of the potential vulnerability resulting from low foreign reserves, it organized a major effort to provide sufficient financing to ensure its credibility. While in the 1990s there is a definite trend in the world economy towards increased flexibility of exchange rate arrangements, the view at the beginning of 1990s was somewhat different. At the beginning of 1990, there was a growing opinion, reflected also at the International Monetary Fund that "the enthusiasm for devaluation and active exchange rate policy has gone too far. It has been pointed out that by relying too heavily on exchange rate adjustments, and by allowing countries to adopt administered systems characterized by frequent small devaluations, many adjustment programs have become excessively inflationary." Edwards (1993, p.2). Since transition economies were generally considered to be inflationary prone, to move towards greater rigidity of exchange rate regime was seen as a way to provide discipline into their macroeconomic and financial systems.

For a peg at least some convertibility of the koruna was required. There was a considerable risk that strong demand of the residents for foreign exchange when currency had no internal convertibility would lead residents to try to get foreign currency from unofficial sources, driving up the unofficial exchange rate. This could potentially undermine the policy of using the official exchange rate as a nominal anchor; (Polak 1991, p 23). For a discussion how convertibility is connected with the exchange rate regimes see among others Williamson (1991) and Hrncir (1993). Limited convertibility of the koruna was introduced on 1 January, 1991.

Thus the decision was made to opt for a fixed exchange rate regime with the goal to use this regime as an important instrument of macroeconomic stabilization. A peg as a nominal anchor may not be feasible if domestic agents believe that this policy will be abandoned if the costs of maintaining it are too high. Thus, clearly the degree of government's commitment to the regime matters. It is interesting to see in this respect that while the commitment of the government was widely perceived as credible, "the authorities did not commit themselves to any pre-announced period of keeping the exchange rate unaffected."; (Hrncir, 1993, p.28). From January 1991, the koruna was pegged to a basket of currencies in a 1 per cent band. The structure of the basket was DEM 45.52%, USD 31.34%, ATS 12.35%, CHF 6.55%, GBP 4.24% from December 1990 until January 1, 1992. From January 2, 1992 until May 2 1993: USD 49.07%, DEM 36.15%, ATS 8.07%, CHF 3.79%, FRF 2.92%. From May 3 1993 until May, 26 1997 the basket was simplified only to include DEM 65% and USD 35%; (Dedek 1997, p. 32).This regime survived until February 1996 when the band was widened from one to fifteen per cent. In May 1997, after a speculative attack, a managed float was introduced.

After deciding on the exchange rate regime, the next step (which was actually occurring simultaneously) was to decide the level at which the currency should be pegged to other currencies. In the 1980s the official exchange rate was administratively controlled and rather stable, but there were also various parallel and black exchange rates. Hrncir (1993) provides evidence that at the end of 1980s the official exchange rate was around 16 koruna for a dollar, the exchange rate at black market approached 35-40 korunas for a dollar. The high rate at a black market reflected also the demand for foreign exchange for asset holding to hedge against possible high inflation.

It was necessary to balance two risks. One risk was that an overly depreciated exchange rate would increase the size of an initial price jump after the price liberalization that coincided with the introduction of the peg, and provide a strong impetus to inflation, making subsequent stabilization more difficult and costly. On the other side, a too small initial devaluation posed a risk that the fixed exchange rate regime would not enjoy sufficient credibility because it would quickly result in a current account deficit that could not be sustained. To make things more complicated, large real shocks to the traditional trading partners and dramatic changes in regional distribution of exports and imports increased the uncertainty about future trade balance development. These real shocks added to the uncertainty about the exchange rate that would be consistent with long-term balance of payments sustainability, and that would at the same time minimize the risk of introducing into the economy an excessive inflation via higher import prices and reduced discipline from foreign competition.

In choosing the initial parity at which to peg the koruna, the authorities ultimately decided to undervalue. Brada and Drabek (1998) argue that this undervaluation of koruna worked as protection through tariffs since it shielded domestic firms from import and gave extra incentives to exporters. Brada and Kutan (1997, p. 109) argue "a large devaluation served to reduce pressures for restructuring in industry, because, with a cheap koruna, more Czech firms in a greater range of sectors were able to export on a profitable basis. The long-term costs may be that investment flows will be directed toward sectors that compete mainly on price rather than on quality, innovation, and other firm-specific advantages, thus trapping the country in a low-wage, low-skill competitive strategy." The pegged exchange rate regime which was introduced from the beginning of 1991 was in 1990 supported by three considerable devaluations of the koruna with the aim to introduce a 'devaluation cushion'. In the beginning of January 1990 an unified commercial rate was established at 15 Czechoslovak koruna (CSK) per dollar, while a separate tourist rate of 38 CSK/$ was still kept. In the summer 1990 the tourist rate was realigned to 23 CSK/$. In October 1990 the commercial rate was raised to 24 and tourist rate to 30 CSK/$. Towards the end of 1990 the tourist rate was abolished and a unified rate of 28 CSK/$ was introduced. In other words the koruna was devalued by 16.6% on January 8, by 55.3% on October 15 and by 15.9% on

December 28 1990. Hrncir (1993, p. 14) argues that the first two devaluations represented more-or-less administrative corrections of the existing exchange ratios, rather than proper devaluations, since they were implemented as isolated acts without price liberalization. Oblath (1994) argues that other factors being equal, the further an economy has been from an open trade regime and the more radical is the trade liberalization, the larger is the necessary initial devaluation. The ratio of official to purchasing power parity exchange rate after these devaluations was approximately three to one; Hrncir (1993). Policy makers hoped that tight fiscal and monetary policies would keep inflationary effects of devaluation in check, while minimizing the risk that the parity would be set on a highly appreciated, and therefore less credible and potentially unsustainable level. In the next section we evaluate the success of this policy.

How Successful Was the Peg in Curbing Inflation?

A comprehensive liberalization of prices was implemented in January 1991. This covered goods that made up approximately 80-90 percent of GDP. Price regulations were still in effect for some rents, energy, municipal services and for products in some monopolized sectors. This of course means that the government kept some control on the initial price shock. For a discussion, see Brada and Kutan (1997, pp.104-106). Monthly data on inflation illustrate that as the effect of price liberalization there was a considerable rise in prices in the first quarter of 1991. However, already in the second quarter of 1991 the rate of inflation has declined significantly. A factor which played an important role was that the government had a clear political support, thus it had a window of opportunity to conduct rapid successful stabilization even if costs in real terms would be unthinkable under "normal" conditions.

In the after-stabilization period, with the exception of administered price increases and the introduction of the value added tax, the rate of inflation remained relatively stable throughout the period of the exchange rate peg. However, inflation could be kept relatively low for a variety of reasons, and thus we attempt to evaluate the role of nominal exchange rate anchor in curbing inflation. For this purpose we use a simple model. In deriving the model and then in estimating it we draw heavily on Edwards (1993).

Consider an economy which produces two types of goods: tradables and non-tradables. Tradable prices are determined at international markets, while non-tradables at domestic markets, which are assumed to clear instantly. In this stylized economy exchange rate is not fixed, and is adjusted to lagged inflation differentials. Wages depend on adjusted previous and expected inflation. The model is then as follows:

$$\pi_t = \alpha\pi_{Tt} + (1-\alpha)\pi_{NTt}$$

This equation says that the domestic price level (π_t) is a weighted average of tradables inflation (π_{Tt}) and non-tradables inflation (π_{Nt}).

$$\pi_{Tt} = E_{t-1}(e_t + \pi_t^*)$$

This equation states that the rate of change of the price of tradables in domestic currency in period t is equal to the expected change in the exchange rate (e_t) plus the expected rate of world inflation (π_t^*).

$$e_t = \phi(\pi_{t-1} - \pi_{t-1}^*)$$

This equation describes the rate of devaluation as an adjusted by a proportion of ϕ to the previous period differential between domestic and world rate inflation.

$$N^D(\frac{P_N}{P_T}, z_t) = N^S(\frac{W}{P_N})$$

This describes the market clearing condition for non-tradables, i.e. the demand for non-tradables is a function of its relative price (P_N / P_T) and of aggregate demand (z_t), and the supply of non-tradables is a function of real wage in this sector.

$$w_t = \gamma\pi_{t-1} + (1-\gamma)\pi_t^e$$

The last equation describes the wage process. The rate of change in wages (w_t) depends on lagged inflation (π_{t-1}) and expected inflation (π_t^e).

To solve the model we assume that inflationary expectations are rational, thus $\pi_t^e = \pi_t + \mu$ where μ is a random disturbance term. Also for convenience we assume that $E_{t-1}(\pi_t^*) = \pi_{t-1}^*$, i.e. that expected world inflation equals the world inflation in the previous period. Thus, we obtain the following:

$$\pi_t = \alpha\pi_{t-1} + \beta\pi_{t-1}^* + \gamma\dot{z}_t + \mu'$$

In this equation coefficient α measures the degree of inertia of domestic inflation. The closer is α to unity the more persistent the inflation will be, the higher will be the degree of inertia in inflation. Edwards (1993, p.7) notes that if α=1, the system has no clear nominal anchor and inflation contains unit root. The relatively stable Czech inflation rate does not seem to contain unit root, and this was confirmed also by statistical tests. Indeed, we tested the null of having a unit root for the consumer price index in levels as well as in log first difference using augmented Dickey-Fuller statistics for the quarterly data for the period 1990:1-1997:4. ADF test statistics using 4 lags was 0.38 for the level and –7.33 for the first difference. This suggests that at 5 per cent significance level CPI index in level contains while first log difference does not contain unit root. In order to investigate empirically the way in which the nominal exchange rate anchor affected the degree of inflationary inertia we estimate the following type of equation using quarterly data for the period 1990:1 - 1997:4.

$$\pi_t = b_0 + b_1\pi_{t-1} + b_2(D\pi_{t-1}) + b_3\pi_{t-1}^* + b_4\dot{z}_{t-1} + u_t$$

where π^*_t is the world rate of inflation, D is a dummy that takes the value of one for the period when the nominal exchange anchor is in place (from 1991:1 until 1997:2) and zero otherwise, and z_t is an index of aggregate macroeconomic policies. If the nominal anchor was perceived as adequate and credible, the coefficient b_2 should be negative and statistically significant at reasonable levels. We approximate z_t by the growth of domestic credit, and world inflation by German consumer price index. Results of the OLS estimation are presented in Table 5 below. In each equation the coefficient b_2 was negative and significant at the ten percent level. This suggests that the nominal anchor program was effective in changing the dynamics of inflation in the Czech Republic. It also suggests that the public perceived the policy as rather credible. These results also indicate a low degree of persistence in Czech inflation. In comparison, similar equations estimated in Edwards (1993) for Mexico, Chile and Yugoslavia yielded significant point estimates of b_1 in the range of 0.75-0.85. The results did not change significantly if we included a dummy for wage control. Income policy especially at the beginning of the period included some rather drastic limits in wage rate indexation, but of course some degree of wage flexibility was still maintained. Brada and Kutan (1997, p.98) present a different opinion. They argue that "the exchange rate has not been a nominal anchor; rather, it has been set so low as to make fighting inflation a relatively secondary issue." However, on page 115 they argue that "the devaluation maneuver must be judged as a success in that the government's objectives were met to the extent that the devaluation was sufficiently large to cushion the effect of the price liberalization, and inflation was reined in so that the nominal exchange rate established in 1991 has easily been maintained.".

In summary, the results presented support the positive role the nominal anchor played in curbing the inflation rate in the Czech Republic during the period 1990-1997. However, as we show in the following sections, we have to take the claim about the success of exchange rate stabilization with an ounce of salt.

Table 5. Regression Analysis. Dependent Variable CPI (π_t)

Variables	constant	π_{t-1}	$D\pi_{t-1}$	π^*_t	Z_t	Z_{t-1}
Coefficient (Standard Error)	**0.032** (0.008)	0.099 (0.190)	**-0.460** (0.238)	0.304 (0.848)	-0.071 (0.532)	---
Coefficient (Standard Error)	**0.026** (0.008)	0.100 (0.191)	**-0.445** (0.240)	0.295 (0.343)	---	0.068 (0.119)

The time period is 1990:1-1997:4. All equations also include a highly significant dummy for the first quarter of 1991 and zero otherwise. Bold numbers designate statistical significance at 10 percent level.

Towards a Change in Exchange Rate Regime: May 1997

After the break-up of Czechoslovakia we distinguish two periods in the Czech transition process. The first period is characterized with tight fixed exchange rate regime (± 0.5 percent band), continuing capital account liberalization, relatively strict income policy (wage controls were basically maintained from the beginning of the stabilization until July 1995; new private firms and ventures with foreign participation were exempted from these rules) combined with good performance (high growth, balanced budget) and substantial nominal interest rate differentials. This leads to high and volatile capital inflow. High capital inflow puts pressure on monetary policy. M2 monetary targets are usually overshot. Attempts to sterilize the impacts of capital inflows are costly and not fully successful. The higher domestic inflation, given stable foreign prices and pegged regime leads to real exchange rate appreciation and slowly rising current account deficit.

The second period begins in February 1996 when the central bank attempts to ease these pressures by widening the band of a peg from ± 0.5 to ± 7.5 percents. This potentially higher instability of the domestic currency had some impact on capital flow, and indeed there was some outflow of presumably short-term capital. However, softer income policy led to higher real wage increases, and continuing real exchange rate appreciation. Consequently, when the growth slows down, the current account deficit rises to very high levels. The combined effect of high current account deficit, slower economic growth, governmental crisis and possible contagious effects from South-East Asia lead to currency crisis. The fixed exchange rate regime introduced at the beginning of transition survived unchanged till spring 1996 when the band was widened. However, in May 1997 the exchange rate regime was abandoned and managed float was introduced. Below we shortly review the reasons which led to the change of the regime.

There was a variety of factors which played a role in changing the exchange rate arrangement. All these factors also led to speculative attack against koruna in May 1997. It seems that the high current account deficit, slowing down of growth, real exchange rate appreciation, and political instability were the most important factors which led to the change of the regime.

One can ask a more principal question whether a small open economy can keep a fixed exchange rate regime in a modern world for a relatively long time. Countries find it increasingly difficult to build the credibility needed to sustain a durable fixed regime for a long period of time. In the Czech case effort to keep koruna fixed was successful for more than six years, but was crushed by the market after a few days of speculative attack in May 1997. Empirical evidence shows that while a large number of countries attempt to keep a tight pegged regime, only a small number succeeds. See Obstfeld and Rogoff (1995). International evidence shows that the ambitions of Czech policy makers were rather high, i.e. the attempts to keep the currency fixed without realignment for a long time is a task which even a more healthy and stronger western European economies - except the Netherlands and Austria - found exceedingly difficult to accomplish.

Another issue is whether a relatively small country can in principle protect its exchange rate if speculators decide to attack it. Obstfeld and Rogoff (1995, p.8) argue that it is a misperception to deduce from the large volume and trading in foreign exchange markets, that if speculators decide to attack a currency of a small country, the central bank has no way to resist. They argue that most central banks have access to enough foreign exchange reserves to "beat down a speculative attack of *any* [italics in original] magnitude, provided they are willing to subordinate all the other goals of monetary policy. To defend a currency peg, the monetary authorities only need enough resources to buy back the high-powered monetary base, equal to deposits at the central bank plus currency. In practice, of course, a central bank never would need to buy up the entire base to repel a speculative attack. By reducing its monetary base sufficiently, the central bank can raise interest rates to a level so high that speculators will find it prohibitively expensive to go short in the domestic currency." Our calculations show that at the beginning of 1997 the Czech National Bank had on hand enough foreign exchange reserves to buy up approximately 80-90 percent of the monetary base. In addition, the central bank could use some other arrangements to borrow more foreign currency. The problem then is not the technical ability to defend the peg, but rather the consequences of the defense on the rest of the economy.

In the Czech situation some of the negative signs (among others current account deficit, real exchange rate appreciation) send a wrong signal to the market. Investors did not necessarily consider, for example a high current account deficit as a bad sign for the long run development of the Czech economy.

Towards the end of 1996 and in the first quarters of 1997, in all likelihood unsustainable high current account deficit and a considerable slowing down of the growth created an environment in which political instability, contagious effects and shift in expectations led to currency crisis. In the Czech conditions the real exchange rate was overvalued however this judgment is obscured by the difficulty to which base year to compare. Monetary policy became to be rather restrictive approximately twelve-fifteen month before the crisis. The fiscal position was worsening however in an international comparison this worsening was still rather mild. Foreign exchange reserves exhibited a declining tendency before the crisis, but their level at the end of the quarter before the crisis still approximately doubled the level of reserves at the end of 1994.

Finally, we mention some transition specifics which seemed to play a rather negative role in the evolution of the crisis. In the Czech Republic financial intermediation is still dominated mostly by banks. While the role of alternative financial intermediation is increasing, deposits at banks and bank loans are still the main source of financing. Furthermore, large commercial banks are excessively involved in the ownership of private companies, mainly through their role in running voucher privatization funds, and keeping decisive equity stakes in industrial and service state companies. These banks are simultaneously creditors of these companies. This gives inadequate incentives to creditors to force performance improvement in companies and it also weakens the application of bankruptcy laws.

It is a fact, and a success, that financial markets developed with immense speed. It seems, however, that the conservative government was overconfident in the allocative power of basically unregulated financial markets. Financial markets were rather poorly regulated until the currency crisis, and several scandals broke out during 1996 and early 1997 signaling poorly supervised financial institutions. Clearly, in this respect the legal areas were developing much slower than the rest of financial institutions. For example the Securities Commission came to exists only after the currency crisis. Before the crisis the Czech media were full of stories of insider trading and similar activities which largely undermined the belief in the transition process and moved the public opinion away from the ruling coalition.

In summary, worsening of fundamentals combined with growing political instability and the expectations of devaluation, and possible contagion effects intensified the depreciation pressures and activated a speculative attack on the koruna in mid-May 1997.

Initially the Czech Central Bank attempted to endure the depreciation pressures through interest rate increases and foreign exchange intervention. However, approximately after a little more than a week, the central bank decided to change the exchange rate arrangement. The decision to abandon the peg before the position of the central bank was compromised helped to build an early return to relative exchange rate stability. It seems to us that even without the speculative attack it was exceedingly difficult to keep the peg. This seems to be also the opinion of the former prime minister [see Klaus 1997] who later argued that the devaluation and the change of the exchange rate regime should have happened approximately one year before the crisis.

After the currency crisis market calmed down rather quickly, interest rates landed softly. Market perceived the efforts of the central bank as adequate, thus the crisis of confidence did not persist for a longer period of time and did not spread to neighboring countries. In June 1997, the government adopted additional budgetary cuts, also a current account somewhat improved in the third quarter of 1997. However, the description of these issues is beyond the scope of this section.

Banking and Exchange Rate Policy in Hungary in the 1990s

This section is a revised version of my lecture in the Institute for Advanced Studies Vienna, Conference on Hungary and EU Eastern Enlargement, June 2002.

In Hungary from 1997 onwards the real GDP is growing around 4 percent trend line. Robust export performance and strong domestic demand drive the growth. After considerate effort inflation is down well below 10%, but there is still a certain disappointment with this performance, especially in view of the Maastrich criteria.

In the way towards the accession to the European Union the role of the banking sector and the exchange rate policy is in the spotlight. Hungary has performed a successful reform of the banking sector. Today it seems to be a generally accepted opinion that – given the limitations of a transition country – Hungary's banking sector functions well. Well-functioning banking sector helps to enforce corporate control and hard budget constraints. Also it seems that effective regulation and supervision of the banking and financial sector helps to moderate the potential vulnerabilities and avoids unnecessary risk-taking in the presence of heavy capital inflows.

During transition Hungary introduced three exchange rate regimes, an adjustable peg, then crawling peg, and currently (from October 2001) Hungary's exchange rate regime is a target zone with wide band of ± 15 per cent, where the parity is determined in relation to euro.

In the period 1990-94 Hungary – as some other transition economies – relied on a more fixed exchange rate regime, however, the adjustable peg with numerous re-alignments fulfilled only in a limited degree the role of nominal anchor. Later the crawling peg made it easier to bring down inflation to a single digit level. However, in order to bring the inflation down further to the levels comparable to the EU-member countries Hungarian authorities were facing a challenge to design an appropriate policy in this direction. Ultimately, the country abandons the crawling peg and moves towards a more flexible target zone regime, and towards a monetary policy framework of inflation targeting.

In this section we describe the evolution of the Hungarian banking sector and then we describe the development of the exchange rate policy.

Hungarian Banking Sector

Some recent contributions in the literature discuss the relationship between financial development and economic growth. See Levine (1996) for a review, and Berglof and Bolton (2001) for an application to transition countries. Empirical work has documented in a cross-country framework that there exists a robust positive correlation between financial intermediation – measured by the ratio of bank lending to GDP, and/or the ratio of stock market turnover to GDP – and growth. Well functioning banking system has a positive impact on medium- and long-term growth. In the last years real growth performance of Hungary was – at least to a certain extent – shaped by the well-functioning banking sector.

In the spring of 2002 Hungary has one of the most stable banking systems in the transition countries. This is due to the successful consolidation, re-capitalization and privatization of the banking sector, which created a right set of incentives for the future behavior of economic actors. Consolidation and re-capitalization of the banking industry had placed considerable burden and privatization led to sizeable revenues for the government budget.

Initially, at the early 1990s, an early boost in the stock market activity, influence of Anglo-Saxon economic thinking, and the early banking crisis created a belief that the financial system of transition countries may emerge along the Anglo-Saxon lines. However, today primarily foreign owned commercial banks dominate the Hungarian financial system, and enterprises rely to a large extent on internally generated resources, and the greater part of long-term finance originates from foreign direct investment. This suggest that the Hungarian financial system seems to develop along the lines of the 'bank-based' system – closer to the German or Austrian model – than along the lines of the Anglo-Saxon 'market-based' system. However, note that empirical evidence is inconclusive concerning the effect of these different financial systems on the growth performance, thus one cannot make easily a positive or negative comment on this tendency.

There are different possible explanations why bank-based system was preferred to market-base system. One explanation may be the cultural and geographical proximity to Germany or Austria. Berglof and Bolton (2001) link the pre-dominance of the bank-based system to the level of development, when they argue that "it is only at more advanced stages of development that one sees financial markets, including stock and bond markets, play an increasingly important role." Berglof and Bolton (2001, p. 26). They provide two sets of reasons for the pre-dominance of bank-based system at the initial stage of development. Both have certain validity for the case of Hungary. First, market based system will develop especially in an environment in which protection of creditor-rights is developed and enforced, and where small investors cannot be exploited by stock exchange manipulators. Until these conditions are fulfilled small investors would feel much more protected by putting their savings into banks than in the stock exchange. Second, in a less developed small open economy, it may happen that nearly all companies will find it too costly to issue bonds or shares in a stock exchange. "Only the more advanced economies have a sufficient number of large and stable firms that could get cheaper funds by issuing securities and thus create the thick market externalities necessary to sustain efficient stock markets." Berglof and Bolton (2001, p. 27).

The pre-dominance of the bank-based system is also the fact for other Central and Eastern European countries, as Poland, Czech Republic, and Slovakia. According to Wagner and Iakova (2001) the banking sector assets in these Central and Eastern European countries account approximately for 85-95 per cent of overall financial assets, in comparison to 50% or so in the United Kingdom. In all of these countries "bank monitoring plays a more important role in corporate governance as opposed to the threat of hostile takeovers, which may characterize more market-based systems. Claims on banks are more important in household portfolios than securities. Thus, banks dominate the provision of financial services." Wagner and Iakova (2001, p. 6).

In support of the thesis that the Hungary's financial system is developing across the lines of the bank-based model one can mention the conditions in the bond market. Bond market capitalization is around 30 percent of GDP compared to about 100 percent of GDP in Western Europe. Hungarian government issues most of the bonds, and the corporate bond market is very small.

Despite the fact that country develops along the lines of the bank-based system, the assets of the banking system as a percentage of GDP are relatively low as compared to some western countries. Credit extended to corporate and household sector accounts approximately to 25 % of GDP in Hungary as compared with more than 100 percent in the United Kingdom. But this ratio is rising currently in Hungary. There are several factors, which may explain the low level of credit to GDP. Credit to households is relatively low simply due to low level of household incomes, which increases bank's lending risk. Also foreign direct investment and privatization lead to high foreign participation of multinational enterprises, which prefer borrowing from their mother companies or from foreign financial institution rather than from resident Hungarian banks.

There was a sharp decline in credit to GDP ratio from 1990 till 1996. However, the initial number of 1990 is hardly comparable with the remaining data, since this may be what Berglof and Bolton (2001) call "accounting fiction." One sees however, in the second half of the 1990s a steady expansion of credit, and one may expect an increase in the financial depth in the future. This may be due to the increase of exchange rate risk (wider exchange rate band from May 2001), which may stimulate resident Hungarian companies to borrow in a larger extent from resident Hungarian banks and thus decrease the risk factor. However, the strong presence of the multinational firms in Hungary, who rely to a large extent on borrowing from their mother companies or mother countries probably explains the fact that the financial depth will stay lower (but somewhat rising) than is typical in some western countries.

More risky participants in the financial markets (households and small and medium size companies) have quite limited access to these markets. However, we observe that markets for these participants expand as mortgage lending, household loans and financing of small and medium size companies grow.

On the deposit side the concentration in the banking sector is very high, while it is lower in the credit side of the market. Competition is steadily growing in the banking sector. This may be documented by declining spreads, shift in bank portfolios from government securities to private sector lending and by declining bank profitability. Interest margins are somewhat higher than in the EU average, and they are decreasing. Berglof and Bolton (2001, p. 42) publish data on loan-deposit rate spreads for transition economies. In 1999 this spread was lowest, 3.4%, in Hungary. Loan rate spread is defined as the average rate charged by commercial banks on outstanding short term credits to enterprises and individuals, weighted by loan amount. Deposit rate is defined as the average rate offered by commercial banks on short term deposits, weighted by deposit amounts. Corresponding data for Latvia was 9.2%,

Czech Republic 4.2%, Sweden 3.9%, U.S.A. 2.7%. It may be that competition leads to decreasing numbers of banks; in 2001 the Kereskedelmi and Hitel Bank and ABN Amro merged to form the second largest bank in Hungary.

Stages of Development of Banking Sector in Hungary

Hungary similarly to other transition economies followed what Bonin and Wachtel (1999, p.3) call the three stages development of banking sectors in transition economies. "The first is the establishment of commercial banks as joint stock companies and of a central bank from the Soviet-era mono banks. The second is the restructuring of bank portfolios and the recapitalization of the banks. The third step, privatization, involves a transfer of ownership from government." We briefly discuss these stages of banking development.

As in other transition economies Hungarian banking system has developed from the domestic mono-bank, which – under socialist regime – was responsible for both the monetary and exchange rate policy as well as for commercial banking activities. The transformation of this system, i.e. the first stage began in Hungary relatively early. In difference to some other transition economies, the state bank system began to be transformed into a two-tier banking system already during the socialist period (note Hungary joined the International Monetary Fund already in 1982). The new banking system introduced in 1987 consisted of the central bank (National Bank of Hungary) and five state-owned commercial banks. Three of these commercial banks – adopting a portion of the central bank's portfolio – were established in 1987 with clients along sector-lines, while the two other commercial banks (the National Savings Bank, OTP, and the Hungarian Foreign Trade Bank) were always present during the socialist period. While originally these banks were heavily under-capitalized with substantial bad-loan portfolio they still provided a pre-transition experience with the two-tier banking system.

The second stage involves restructuring of bank portfolios and recapitalization of banks. These steps were needed because, despite initial pro-reform steps, the banking sector got into deep crisis in the beginning of the transition. There was a mixture of reasons, which led to the initial crisis. Describing the main causes of the crisis we draw on Szapary (2001) and Tang, Zoli and Klytchnikova (2000). First, the initial fall of output and income at the beginning of transition led to bankruptcies of bank clients. Furthermore, high real interest rates, early inflation of around thirty per cent, and an increase in inter-enterprise credit aggravated this situation. Second, Hungarian state banks dealt with a large volume of non-performing loans, which were mostly the legacy of the direct lending under the socialist system, but also the share of non-performing loans was increasing in the first years of transition. Third, credit market was segmented along sector-lines, which had negative impact on competition. Fourth, there were considerable shortcomings in supervision. Szapary (2001) writes that at the early beginning of transition, until the new laws were accepted, the valid regulation and rules for loan classification and provisions did not compel the banks to practice prudent lending and to make adequate loan loss provisions. The change has occurred towards the end 1991 when various new laws were accepted by the legislation concerning the financial institutions, accounting procedures, taxing procedure, and bankruptcy. Bonin and Schaffer (1999) provide an interesting retrospective look at Hungary's experience with what they call "a particularly draconian bankruptcy law". Berglof and Bolton (2001, p. 12) speak about "a devastatingly effective bankruptcy law."

Initially, the new commercial banks remained under state ownership as well as their business clients, so lending policies were not based on strict financial or economic logic; Berglof and Bolton (2001, p.5). Hungarian government intervened by replacing bad loans with government bonds, but at this initial stage there was not a clear understanding that a radical change is also needed in operations and management of these banks. As conditions got stricter and recapitalization was followed by privatization the situation got better. Szapary (2001).

The process of bank consolidation involved combination of different measures. Initially portfolio cleaning of the banks and then enterprise-oriented portfolio cleaning was attempted. "Those banks and savings cooperatives which had a capital adequacy ratio of less than about 7 percent were given government bonds in exchange for their non-performing loans at the end of 1992. ... A part of the bad loans was sold by the government at a discount to the Hungarian Development Bank (HDB). HDB is a state owned asset management agency working with government guarantees, which had responsibility for the collection of bad assets. But HDB was not very successful in the recovery of assets since it had not a clear mandate, not enough power and also it was rather passive agency and not an active asset portfolio manager. (Wagner and Iakova, 2001 p. 20). Another part of the bad loans was left with the banks to be worked out. ... Those loans that could not be worked-out or sold [to private work-out companies] were handed over to the HDB, which in many cases had to write off the debt." Szapary, (2001, p.10).

Recapitalization (the increase in the capital adequacy ratio of the four large state-owned banks to 8 percent, and in other banks to 4 percent) was implemented in 1993-1994. This was done mainly by government purchasing – through issuing bonds – newly issued shares of these re-capitalized banks, and by extending loans to these banks. The consolidation of the Hungarian banking system had come to an end towards 2000.

Whether cost of bank restructuring was high or low depends on international comparison, since probably no other metric is available. Szapary (2001) considers these costs relatively low in international comparison, especially if one compares it with the cost of bank consolidation in South-East Asia after the crisis of 1997. Ultimately, the increase of the foreign ownership in the Hungarian banking system stabilized the Hungarian banking system.

Hungary privatized its banking sector primarily by means of sales to foreign investors who were able to inject additional capital into these banks. This process started relatively slowly in the beginning of the 1990s, but with the exception of Postabank and OTP to a large extent finished at the end of 1997. Here, one should note that before the large-scale privatization of Hungarian banks began, the foreign banks were already present on the Hungarian market. Varhegyi (2001, p. 582) shows that at the beginning of the 1990s one finds foreign banks on the Hungarian market. These included ABN Amro, BNP, Commerzbank, Creditanstalt, Credit Lyonnais, Daewoo, Dresdner Bank, HypoVereinsbank, ING, Nomura and Volksbank. In addition, some small-scale bank privatization had already begun too, as the case of Westdeutsche Landesbank, and Hanwha documents. Foreign bank incentives to enter Hungarian market seem to be twofold. First, there was a need to provide services to their (multi-national) customers who entered Hungarian market. Second, the less developed Hungarian market provided distinct profit opportunities. Varhegyi (2001, p. 584) mentions that profit opportunities were effectively used especially by Austrian banks as CA and Raiffeisen. Postabank required a major government bail-out in 1998. "Some weaknesses of supervision were revealed in 1998 when two of the privatized banks – Postabank and

Realbank – failed, although problems with their operations were known to supervisors well ahead of the failures. ... After renationalizing Postabank in the wake of its collapse, the government had planned to reprivatize it after restructuring. In the event, the government granted exclusive negotiating rights to OTP, Hungary's largest domestically-owned bank. But OTP's offer for Postabank was deemed too low, so the government has now decided to keep it in state hands by selling it to the state-owned Hungarian Post." (Wagner and Iakova, 2001, p. 59).

The first bank privatization occurred in the middle of 1994, and by the end of 1997, the state owned only around 20 % of total bank assets in Hungary, and foreigners owned 62%, up from 12 % in 1994. Bonin and Wachtel (1999, p. 12), and Varhegyi (1999). The increased presence of foreign investors in the Hungarian banking sector was also a result of liberal licensing policy. Currently only one large and one small commercial bank and a few credit institutions fulfilling special functions [Eximbank, the Hungarian Development bank among others] remain in the state ownership. Foreign ownership amounts to more than 60 percent of the share capital of the banking system. Szapary (2001, pp. 15-16).

The evaluation of the Hungarian banking system especially after successful privatization of state-owned banks to strategic investors is very positive. Wagner and Iakova (2001, p.16) write: "Currently, Hungary has one of the most modern and advanced financial systems among the transition economies."

Hungarian Exchange Rate Policy

The observation – that in transition economies various exchange rate regimes seem to work – may had led the European authorities to their current position concerning the exchange rate arrangements of these countries. Position of the European authorities seems clear: till these countries join the EU there are no restrictions on the choice of their exchange rate regime; an exception maybe an earlier introduction of euro (euroization). Hungary as well as any other pre-accession country will first enter the EU and the ERM Two (exchange rate mechanism which gets into force before EMU but after EU membership), Exchange Rate Mechanism Two determines a bilateral relation between a member currency and the euro. Central parity towards the euro is determined jointly with the ECB and the band may be of ± 15%, although narrower band is in principle also possible, if ECB agrees. Realignment of the central rate is possible by agreement with the ECB. But the Maastricht criterion on exchange rate stability requires that currency is kept for two years between normal fluctuation margins without re-alignment and only later joins the EMU and adopt the euro. Theoretically, there is a possibility to adopt the euro earlier by unilateral euroization. In contrast to Poland, this issue does not seem to be much scrutinized in Hungary. Joining the European Monetary Union will be the final phase of the process towards integration.

We distinguish three basic periods in the evolution of Hungarian exchange rate policy in transition.

The first is the period from the beginning of transition till the introduction of the adjustment program in March 1995. In the first period the exchange rate regime is an adjustable peg, characterized with numerous realignments.

The second period runs from March 1995 till May 2001. In this period the exchange rate regime is a crawling peg with pre-announced devaluation and narrow band.

The third period begins in May 2001 and runs till today. In this period, first the crawling peg was kept till October 2001, but the band was considerably widened, and the rate of pre-announced devaluation decreased. Finally, in October 2001 the pre-announced devaluation was abandoned. Currently the Hungarian exchange rate regime is a target zone with ±15 % band.

Hungary's decision in the beginning of the 1990s to introduce fixed but adjustable exchange rate reflected the approach prevailing at the beginning of transition to treat fixed exchange rate as a nominal anchor. Halpern and Nemenyi (1999, p. 432) write "targeting monetary aggregates was not feasible." However, in difference for example to the Czech Republic Hungarian fixed exchange rate did not perform well in its anchoring function. In the period from January 1990 till March 1995 the forint was devalued twenty-two times on a discretionary basis. Szapary and Jakab (1998, p. 881) write that these devaluations were typically a reaction to inflationary and balance of payments developments. The exchange rate band increased somewhat but was still kept very tight. Exchange-rate adjustments were directed by considerations of containing inflation, and maintaining competitiveness of the tradable sector; Halpern and Nemenyi (1999, p. 432), Szapary and Jakab (1998, p. 878). This type of exchange rate policy encouraged speculation against the domestic currency, and under-mined the credibility of the central bank. Szapary and Jakab (1998, p. 881) write that the speculation about new possible devaluation began immediately after the last devaluation had occurred. This was done by delaying of repatriation of foreign currency earned from export or earlier invoicing in imports. As it is typically the case in the pegged but adjustable regime, policy makers postpone devaluation, and then devalue less than the market calls for. The National Bank of Hungary has also acknowledged this loss. "In the end, 1994 monetary policy failed to obtain its basic economic goals" National Bank of Hungary Annual Report 1994, quoted from Golinelli and Rovelli (2001, p.6).

Table 6. Official Devaluation of the HUF; January 1990 – February 1995

	In percentage		In percentage
31. January 1990	1.0	06. February 1990	2.0
20. February 1990	2.0	07. January 1991	15.0
08. November 1991	15.8	16. March 1992	1.9
24. June 1992	1.6	09. November 1992	1.9
12. February 1993	1.9	26. March 1993	2.9
07. June 1993	1.9	09. July 1993	3.0
29. September 1993	4.5	03. January 1994	1.0
16. February 1994	2.6	13. May 1994	1.0
10. June 1994	1.2	05. August 1994	8.0
11. October 1994	1.1	29. November 1994	1.0
03. January 1995	1.4	14. February 1995	2.0

Source: National Bank of Hungary, homepage.

Table 7. Changes in the Width of the HUF band

From 01.07. 1992	± 0.3 %
From 01.06. 1994	± 0.5 %
From 05.08. 1994	± 1.25%
From 22.12. 1994	± 2.25%

Source: National Bank of Hungary, homepage.

At the beginning of the 1990s – in difference to some other transition economies – Hungary faced a relatively high level of external debt. In 1990 the ratio of the gross debt to gross domestic product was around 70 %. Thus in addition to 'transition' issues Hungarian policy makers were also to avoid possible debt crisis. Government policies were successful in a sense that they avoided the debt crisis, however, the partially chaotic exchange rate policy may be a consequence of it. Szapary and Jakab (1998, p. 880) confirm this view by arguing that while it would be possible to fix the forint in the early 1990s, but that would endanger the competitiveness of the economy. This view reflected the experience of the 1980s, where balance of payment problems were typically tackled by adjusting the value of the forint, which after some lag appeared as inflationary pressure in the domestic economy.

Inflationary inertia was difficult to contain. Twenty percent and higher inflation prevailing in 1992 to 1994 had two sources: inertia of expectations and the Ricardo-Harrod-Balassa-Samuelson effect. "While due to the increasing competition the tradable prices have become determined increasingly by the world market prices and the exchange rate, the productivity and wage increase in the tradable sector influenced the non-tradable wages, which notwithstanding, added some further impetus to inflation." (Halpern and Nemenyi 1999, p. 432). Consumer price index was over 30 per cent in 1991, then decreased for two consecutive years and again climbed up in 1994. The ratio of budget and current account deficit to the gross domestic product were both approaching ten percent of gross domestic product, and there were signs of continuation of this process. There was also an increase in the ratio of gross and net foreign debt to gross domestic product. Market expected further devaluation of the forint, and short-term outflow of capital was noticed. As the Central Bank document itself stated, "in the wake of several unexpected devaluations the earlier fixed, but adjustable exchange rate regime lost its credibility." Monetary Policy in Hungary, (May 2000, p. 54). As a result in March 1995 an adjustment stabilization package was designed and introduced. For an in-depth analysis of the pre-1995 period see Suranyi and Vincze (1998), Halpern and Nemenyi (1999), and Szapary and Jakab (1998).

The 1995 stabilization program involved an introduction of a new exchange rate regime. Crawling peg was to play the role of the nominal anchor to influence inflationary expectations, thus possibly decreasing inflation at relatively low real costs. Hungarian policy makers rightly wanted to influence inflationary expectations, and to put a brake on the inflationary inertia. Gacs (2000) connects the emergence of inertia of inflationary expectations already with the socialist period. Note that in the 1980s the consumer price inflation rate was on average around 10%. In Box 1 below we consider some empirical evidence which may suggest a long-memory inflationary inertia.

Box 1: Hungary and the Czech Republic in Long-Run Perspective

Monetary processes may have long memories. In this respect Hungary – looking at the experience of the 20th century – seems to be a country with relatively easy money policy. At least this can be documented comparing the behavior of Hungarian currency to the Czech (Czecho-Slovak) currency during the last century. Exposed to similar shocks Czechoslovakian (and subsequently Czech and, to a somewhat lesser extent, Slovak) policy makers were typically able to keep the domestic currency stable. For example, while the exchange rate was equal in 1913 (both territories belonged to the same political unit), in 1920 we find the value of Czechoslovak koruna at 1.60, while Hungarian korona at 0.201 (US cents of contemporary gold content per unit of currency). In 1925 these values change to 2.97 and 0.0014 respectively. See M.C. Kaser ed. The Economic History of Eastern Europe 1919-1975, Clarendon Press, Oxford, 1985, p. xii. Similarly in the transition period, in 1991 29.56 Czechoslovak korunas equals one dollar, while 74.73 forints. In 1998 the two values are 32.29 and 214.40, respectively. Source: Fidrmuc, Fidrmuc, Horvath (2002)

The 1995 adjustment program helped to re-instate – at least in the short run – the fiscal discipline. The outright devaluation of the forint by 9 per cent was to increase competitiveness of the tradable sector. The intention was that the crawling peg with pre-announced devaluation scheme enables to regain the lost credibility of the previous period. There was clearly a need for such a step, since to regain the credibility of monetary authorities – after the bleak performance of the previous regime – was a must. Szapary and Jakab (1998, p. 882) write the central bank and the government announced the monthly devaluation rate of the crawling peg couple of weeks before the rate became to be effective so that the market agents had sufficient time period to adjust.

There was a shift in policy makers understanding of the exchange rate policy. In the first period the exchange rate policy was to follow two main priorities: reduction of the rate of inflation and simultaneously to help current account problems. By 1995 it had been recognized that this concept is not sustainable any more. Monetary policy begins to put priority to reduction of inflation.

However, in this regime the independence of the monetary policy has been reduced. Evidently this regime meant a constraint on the central bank's interest rate policy. The gradual liberalization of money and capital markets and the new crawling peg regime led to tighter connections between the domestic and foreign interest rates through uncovered interest rate parity, which reduced the room for the domestic policy makers. "Under the crawling peg regime the central bank's independence in setting interest rates is determined by the exchange rate and the country risk that investors perceive and the width of the exchange rate's fluctuation band. When interest rates fail to coincide with the yields expected by foreign investors – for instance, because of changes in the risk premium – the forint moves within the exchange rate band and eventually, in case of a significant misalignment, foreign exchange intervention evolves at the edges of the fluctuation band."; Monetary Policy in Hungary, May 2000, p. 58.

The introduction of pre-announced crawling peg has made the future exchange rate changes more predictable. The exchange rate has become the nominal anchor in the economy. Table 8 below shows the evolution of the pre-announced devaluation rates.

Table 8. Official Devaluation of the Forint, 1995-2001

	In percentage		In percentage
13. March 1995	9.0; no daily devaluation	16. March 1995 -	1.9; daily devaluation 0.060
29. June 1995 -	1.3; daily devaluation 0.042	02. January 1996 -	1.2; daily devaluation 0.040
01. January 1997-	1.2; daily devaluation 0.040	01. April 1997 -	1.1; daily devaluation 0.036
15. August 1997-	1.0; daily devaluation 0.036	01. January 1998 -	0.9; daily devaluation 0.030
15. June 1998-	0.8; daily devaluation 0.026	01. October 1998	0.7; daily devaluation 0.023
01.January 1999-	0.6; daily devaluation 0.02	01. July 1999	0.5; daily devaluation 0.0163
01. October 1999-	0.4; daily devaluation 0.0133	01. April 2000	0.3; daily devaluation 0.0098
01. April 2001-	0.2; daily devaluation 0.0066	04 May 2001-	0.2; daily devaluation 0.0066
01. October 2001-	no daily devaluation		

Source: National Bank of Hungary. The first number indicates the monthly rate of devaluation.

Szapary and Jakab (1998, p. 883) write that the crucial aspect of the success of the crawling peg regime was the fact that the growth momentum of 1997 – for the first time in the period of twenty years – was not linked with worsening of the balance of payments.

An exchange rate based stabilization program is typically successful if the exchange rate policy is credible and sustainable. This means that the external commitment of the government cannot be in contradiction with its fiscal, income and monetary policy. There was a substantive devaluation of forint in 1995. All in all in the first half of 1995 forint lost around 20 percent, which was sufficient to avoid real appreciation. The projected inflation rate was around 24-26%, the real CPI inflation little bit higher, but sill the scale of devaluation held back worsening of the current account deficit. "Indeed, the depreciation of the forint on the foreign exchange markets was over 5 percentage points less than the official devaluation of the band-centre." Varhegyi (2001, p.4). In 1995 the forint parity devalued by almost 30%, while the market rate approximately by 24%. In 1996 the two measurements of devaluation were approximately equal. Varhegyi (2001, p. 22). Under a relatively fixed exchange rate and free capital mobility the monetary policy is constrained. This means that the interest rate is determined to a certain extent by the implications of the un-covered interest rate parity, and there is not much space for a truly independent interest rate policy. Thus, from the point of view of sustainability of the exchange rate regime the more important become the fiscal and the income policy.

Except for 1998 and to some extent 2000 the fiscal policy was to a large extent consistent with the exchange rate policy. In other words the declining rate of devaluation occurred jointly with decreasing of the share of government expenditures as the percentage of GDP, as well as with the modest rate of growth of public borrowing. Varhegyi (2001, p. 6) writes that "in the most part of the past six years, the budgetary policy did not threaten the sustainability of the announced rate of devaluation through increasing the volume of domestic loans." Growth of wages exceeded the rate of parity devaluation. Varhegyi (2001, p. 6-7) adds that the increase in the growth of wages should be seen in a more positive way if "adjusted by productivity growth, which was 5 per cent in 1993, and an average of 3 per cent in the 1996-2000 period."

Monetary policy – although restrained by the exchange rate regime – also attempted to "slow down the fall in domestic interest rates as much as possible." Varhegyi (2001, p. 6). These higher interest rates than led to speculative capital inflows, which were counter-acted by the central bank sterilization policy. Central Bank typically used passive repo operations to counterbalance the excess liquidity generated by these flows. Szapary and Jakab (1998, p. 895) calculate the costs of sterilization in the period from spring 1995 till the end of 1997. Their calculation estimates the cost in 0.16 per cent of yearly GDP. But while this higher interest rate supported savings it simultaneously led to interest rate premium resulting in capital inflows. These flows were pushing for an appreciation of the currency. This was reflected also in the fact that except for periods of international financial turbulence, forint was moving typically in the appreciated section of the band.

In summary, then it seems that the crawling peg performed well as a nominal anchor, alleviated competitiveness, and helped to increase the credibility of the policy makers. The improved competitiveness of Hungarian economy was to a large extent a result of productivity growth. Since this growth was faster than in most of Hungary's western trading partners the rate of devaluation could lag somewhat behind the inflation differential.

The crawling peg was successful in bringing down the inflation from close to 30 percent to about 10 percent, and also it stabilized inflationary expectations and thus helps to raise the credibility of the National Bank of Hungary. However, the disinflationary process under the crawling peg regime was considered to be quite slow. Single-digit inflation was achieved in the Czech Republic and Slovakia in 1995, in Slovenia in 1996, in Latvia and Lithuania in 1997; Bulgaria, Estonia and Poland in 1999, while in Hungary only in 2000. Gacs (2000, p.7). In addition the disinflation was halted in the second half of 2000. There were different reasons for slowing down of the disinflationary process: inertia in inflationary expectations, volatility of the oil price, depreciation of euro towards dollar, inflationary momentum in food prices and in some non-tradable prices, and finally maybe the exchange rate regime itself.

There were also some other reasons, which contributed to the abandoning of the crawl. Hungarian exchange rate policy coped with capital inflow pressures. These inflows kept the forint at the appreciating section of the band, which pressured the central bank to cut interest rates to weaken the incentives for inflow. However, the loosening of the monetary stance might re-awaken inflation, especially if conditions were tight at some segments of the Hungarian labor market, and if growth was rather significant. Such pressures were sometimes difficult to keep, and were prompting the central bank to increase the rates. "The narrow-band crawling exchange rate regime left very little space for the NBH to maneuver. Sometimes, the central bank was compelled to cut the interest rates even when the economy did not justify such a move. This happened for example in early 2000, when the massive capital inflow got the bank to slash the interest rates, although neither a halt in disinflation nor a dangerously low level of savings warranted this measure. Thus, the monetary policy, losing from its tightness in the inflexible exchange rate regime, became unable to perform the function it was originally designed for, namely to curb inflation." Varhegyi (2001, p. 15). These contradictory tendencies tied the hands of the central bank and – among others – contributed to the atmosphere of a need of change of the regime.

Another reason for the introduction of new exchange rate regime was the change in the leadership of the Central Bank. However, as alluded to already, the strongest reason for abandoning the crawling peg was the fact that Hungary still had comparatively high inflation at the beginning of 2001. The decision was taken to speed up disinflation, and curb the inertia fuelled by inflationary expectations. In order to make easier the management of the higher exchange rate risk, which followed from the wider intervention band, government removed all barriers to the free movement of capital in mid-June 2001.

Box 2: Policy of the NBH after Appointment of the New President

2001

March 2, Zsigmond Járai was appointed president of the National Bank of Hungary (NBH). Decision to reduce the monthly devaluation rate from 0.3 to 0.2 % from April 1, 2001.

May 3, the NBH had widened the exchange rate band in which currency fluctuates against the euro to 15 % while still it retained the 0.2 % monthly rate of crawling peg devaluation. The Central Bank Council declared sustainable reduction of inflation as the principal objective of monetary policy.

June 15, Hungarian government lifted all foreign exchange restrictions and implemented the full convertibility of forint in terms of current as well as capital transactions for both residents as well as non-residents. The earlier legal obligation of repatriating foreign exchange is removed. Hungarian residents can open forint and foreign currency accounts abroad without applying for permission. Foreign currency obtained under any title whatever is permitted to be credited on foreign currency accounts of residents or non-residents. Transactions in foreign currency is allowed in Hungary.

June 12, The NBH has introduced program to attain a price stability (2 % inflation) to fulfill the Maastricht criteria by 2004/2005. The NBH has set the end-2001 target at 7 % and for end-2002 at 4.5 %. To this target the Central Bank has set a 1 % 'tolerance' band on both sides.

June 19, The Hungarian Parliament passed the new Act on the National Bank of Hungary, which complies with the acquis communautaire of the EU. The Law guarantees the independence of the NBH from the Hungarian Government. Personal independence of members of the Bank's decision-making bodies is strengthened under the new law. Members of the Monetary Council, the Bank's supreme decision-making body are appointed for a six year term.

July 13, The interest rates on the Central Bank's instruments are: two-week central bank deposit (central bank base rate) 11.25%; overnight central bank deposit (central bank base rate less 2 percentage points) 9.25%; overnight repo (central bank base rate plus 2 percentage points) 13.25 %.

July 23, Central Bank in the official Evaluation of Monetary Policy Statement states that "since the change in the exchange rate system, the central bank has not made any interest rate changes, but the widening of the band has been followed by an appreciation of the forint. The key factor behind the appreciation has been higher external demand for long term government securities.

August 21, The Monetary Council accepted to abandon the crawling peg devaluation of the forint from 1 October 2001. The central parity was fixed at 276.1 HUF per one euro. Implicit inflation targeting was introduced in which the central parity lost its earlier function of a nominal anchor. The NBH will attempt to guide inflation expectations via a disinflation path (regular inflation forecasts will be publicly available). This will provide market with a nominal anchor to develop expectations.

September 10, The Monetary Council reduced central bank base rate by 25 points. The interest rate on the NBH base rate (two-week central bank deposit) is 11%.

September 24, The Monetary Council was of the opinion that the September 11 terror attack justifies widening of the gap between forint and euro interest rates. Thus, the NBH did not follow ECB in reducing interest rates.

October 24, The Monetary Council reduced central bank base rate by 25 points to 10.75%.

November 13, The Monetary Council reduced central bank base rate by 50 points to 10.25 %

December 11, The Monetary Council reduced central bank base rate by 50 points to 9.75%.

2002

January 7. The Monetary Council reduced central bank base rate by 25 basis points to 9.5%.

January 21, The Monetary Council reduced central bank base rate by 50 basis points to 9%.

February 18, The Monetary Council reduced central bank base rate by 50 basis points

March 18, The Monetary Council has left the central bank base rate unchanged at 8.5%.

April 8, The Monetary Council has left the central bank base rate unchanged at 8.5%.

April 22, The Monetary Council has left the central bank base rate unchanged at 8.5%.

May 21, The Monetary Council has increased the central bank base rate to 9.0%.

This dissatisfaction with the crawling peg led to the introduction of the new exchange rate regime. When deciding on the new exchange rate regime different options were possible from which the policy makers in May 2001 have chosen a wide band around the central parity. One possibility would be a currency board. Tying the hands of the monetary policy-makers seems not to be an option in case of the highly qualified staff and leadership of the Hungarian Central Bank. Furthermore, the trend real appreciation – which seems to be justified by rapid productivity growth – is better accommodated under more flexible regime; Masson (1999, p. 15).

Hungarian Central Bank provided the following explanation for the change of the exchange rate regime. "However, for the past two years, no further reduction has been made in the rate of price increases. Although the factors to blame for this unfavorable situation also included a series of negative inflationary shocks and a higher rate of imported inflation over the past two years, still a more ambitious disinflation policy calls for a more active monetary policy. However, this was not possible under the previous narrow-band exchange rate regime, as the Central Bank had to totally subordinate its interest rate policy to the external developments. In fact, the only freedom left for the Central Bank and the Government lay in setting the rate and date of the pre-announced devaluation. Widening the range within which the exchange rate is allowed to fluctuate will diminish the subjugation of interest rate policy and enable the Central Bank to develop its benchmark rates and hence the exchange rate so that the designated disinflation path can be maintained."; National Bank of Hungary: Statement on the New System of Monetary Policy on June 12, 2001.

This is supported also in the IMF assessment, too. "Directors agreed that the narrow crawling exchange rate band had contributed to Hungary's past successes, but that it had outlived its usefulness. In view of the present and prospective challenges to policy, they welcomed the widening of the band, which should facilitate the central bank's efforts to reduce inflation by providing the necessary leeway to tighten monetary conditions, when needed, including through a moderate appreciation of the forint. Most agreed that a moderate appreciation, if it occurred, would not derail Hungary's strong external competitiveness. Greater exchange rate flexibility would also strengthen the financial system by discouraging speculation and unhedged borrowing." (IMF, 2001 p.3).

This decision to widen the band and to stop the pre-announced devaluation also meant moving away from exchange rate targeting and to look for a more credible way to decrease inflation. A few weeks after the band widening, the NBH announced the introduction of the inflation targeting. As it is known inflation targeting is a monetary policy framework characterized by official announcement of quantitative target ranges or targets for the inflation rate for certain time horizons. It is an important part of the monetary targeting that the central bank makes its plans concerning the inflation publicly available and transparent, and that public is persuaded that stable low inflation (or disinflation) is credibly the goal of the central bank.

One month later the NBH published the inflation target band for the coming 18 months. The targeted inflation rate was 7 percent by the end of 2001, 4.5 percent by the end of 2002, and 3.5 percent by the end of 2003 with a ± 1 percent degree of tolerance.

Inflation targeting gives a policy freedom to policy makers to carry out a more independent monetary policy and allows them to link different policy instruments to the targeted inflation index. The real question about the success of the inflation targeting will depend on the strength of monetary policy makers and their independence from the fiscal framework. There is a certain fear that the expansive fiscal policy, which was a prelude to the election competition in the spring 2002 may continue. Fiscal dominance, which would – in one way or the other – dominate money growth will have negative impact on the success of inflation targeting. The IMF Executive Board Assessment from May 2001 clearly warned that "monetary policy could not by itself achieve both inflation and external objectives, especially in the context of robust economic growth, and that it will be important to have an appropriate fiscal adjustment." (IMF 2001, p.3.) Conservative government (1998-2002) seemed to favor creating a strong state with active fiscal stimuli policy (Széchenyi Plan for example). The same Executive Board Assesment from May 2001: "Directors agreed that a broadly neutral fiscal stance in 2001 and 2002 – which would require a substantial withdrawal of fiscal stimulus relative to that embedded in the budget and in planned off-budget spending – would be appropriate."

Also, it is not clear yet how accurately will be the NBH able to hit the inflation target. As Masson (1999, pp. 18-19) argues it is essential that the policy makers have reliable and generally accepted way of making inflation targeting forecasts 'so as to justify raising interest rates when necessary to preempt potential inflationary pressures that may not be visible in actual inflation data."

The extent to which the new monetary policy framework will succeed in curbing inflation remains to be seen.

As a result of the widening of the band the forint began to appreciate, and it has been 8-12 percent above the parity ever since. This appreciation of the forint was accompanied by the cut of the NBH base interest rate (two-week central bank deposit) from 11.25 to 8.5 per cent from July 2001 till May 2002. In May 2002 the interest rate was increased due to the re-appearance of the inflationary pressures to 9.0 per cent. The introduction of inflation targeting had positive impact on disinflation process. In the first quarter of 2002, the consumer price index decreased to 6.2 per cent compared to 7.2 per cent in the last quarter of 2001. National Bank of Hungary, "Quarterly Report on Inflation," May 2002, p. 14. However, in April 2002 it seems that the process of disinflation was halted.

Reasons for the appreciation of the currency are mainly connected with higher external demand for long term government securities. This increasing demand – among others – may be a consequence of very positive Hungarian credit rating. For example Moody's rating is A3 from November 2000; Standard and Poor's is A- from December 2000, furthermore both rating agencies consider the situation stable. Spreads on sovereign benchmark bonds are among the lowest in the region. Investors' share of holdings of forint-denominated government securities reaches record highs. After reaching the peak of the foreign owned portfolio at the beginning of July 2001 (HUF 1011 billion), it again grew in December 2001 it exceeded HUF 1060 billion. Hungarian Financial Supervisory Authority, "Report on the Development of the Supervised Sectors in the First Three Quarters of 2001," p. 12/26. These flows may become volatile under some unexpected shocks however there seems to be enough space in the wide band to accommodate them.

Potentially a crisis with speculative attack against the forint forcing forint out of the band may occur. This would have an impact on the overall economic situation in the country. This scenario has a relatively low probability. First, current exchange rate arrangement and skills and determination of the NBH to defend the exchange rate regime do not seem to support emergence of any currency crisis. Second, even if such currency crisis occurs the healthiness of the banking sector may protect the economy from becoming it a banking and financial crisis. Gomulka (2001, p.7) quotes Kawalec (1999) who in a comparative study of the banking sector systemic risk assigns to Hungary the lowest score, i.e. the very low risk. Kawalec, S. "Banking Sector Risk in Selected Central European Countries," CASE Report No. 23, Warsaw 1999.

However, there exists a potentiality of what Gomulka (2001) calls mini-crisis. Such crisis may originate in unsuccessful policy mix. Macroeconomic stability may be lost if the policy mix is not sustainable, which for practical reasons – given the independence of the central bank and the current exchange rate regime – means a danger stemming from an unsustainable fiscal policy.

Inflation targeting provides a better defense to potential speculative attacks than adjustable peg, or exchange rate system with narrow bands. However, Masson (1999) reminds us that inflation targeting will boost the credibility of policy makers only if it involves "more than vague commitments to bring inflation down to EU levels." Recent modest speeding up of inflation together with publicly known differences on exchange rate policy and the speed of disinflation between the two political groupings in Hungary may bear potential risks. One may also ask whether the country had already achieved a political consensus in favor of a low inflation, and also whether the central bank has already established a predictable association connecting the policy instruments and the future inflation rate. Evidently, unsuccessful inflation targeting may endanger the credibility of the central bank and consequently it might affect the exchange rate behavior.

As a result of the trend real appreciation and inflation inertia it may be a difficult task for Hungarian policy makers to achieve the Maastricht criteria for inflation. Maastricht nominal convergence criteria require that inflation be no more than 1.5 per cent points above the average inflation of the best three already EU members. The Ricardo-Harrod-Balassa-Samuelson effect implies that the price level may be kept stable only "if the exchange rate appreciates at rate that equals the product of the share of non-traded goods in the price index and the difference in productivity growth in the two sectors." Masson (1999, p. 16). If exchange rate stability is preferred, then consequently the domestic inflation will be higher than the inflation of the foreign countries approximately by the same amount, and this may contradict the Maastricht nominal criteria.

Certain risk stems from the perceived and maybe real contradiction between the real and nominal convergence criteria. Large capital inflows may intensify after enlargement, which may lead to a conflict between the Maastricht Treaty inflation requirements and the pressure stemming from the Ricardo-Harrod-Balassa-Samuelson effect.

The European Union has performed a very vital role in providing outside anchor for the financial and also macroeconomic development of Hungary in the 1990s. The pressure to meet the criteria for the membership in the European Union was essential in adoption and enforcement of laws and regulation important for building the Hungarian financial and banking architecture. The banking sector after consolidation, recapitalization, and privatization has significantly contributed to the hardening of the budget constraint and thus to good real performance of the economy.

In the 1990s the Hungarian exchange rate policy maintained always certain degree of exchange rate flexibility. This flexibility was achieved either through numerous re-aligments of parity under pegged but adjustable regime, or under the pre-announced devaluation rate in the crawling peg regime, and especially by substantial widening of the band in the recently introduced target zone. There were periods when despite this flexibility the forint was for a significant time period at one edge of the band. This was the stylized fact for most of the crawling peg period as it is today during the target zone with wide band. In exchange rate policy some inevitable tensions remain.

REFERENCES

Agenor, Pierre-Richard and Peter J. Montiel, Development Macroeconomics, *Princeton University Press,* 1996.

Aizenman, Joshua and Robert P. Flood, "A Theory of Optimum Currency Areas: Revisited," International Monetary Fund 1992, *Working Paper WP/92/39,* May 1992.

Allen, Polly Reynolds and Peter B. Kenen, Asset Markets, Exchange Rates, and Economic Integration, A Synthesis, *Cambridge University Press,* 1980.

Andreff, Wladimir, "Nominal and Real Convergence – at What Speed?" in Brabant, van J. ed. (1999)

Argy, Victor, "Choice of Exchange Rate Regime for a Smaller Economy: A Survey of Some Key Issues," in Argy, Victor, and Paul de Grauwe, Choosing an Exchange Rate Regime: The Challenge for Smaller Industrial Countries. International Monetary Fund, Katholieke Universiteit Leuven, Macquarie University 1990, 6-81.

Artis, Michael, Marion Kohler, and Jacques Melitz, "Trade and the Number of OCA's in the World," European University Institute, 1998, Economics Department, *Working Paper ECO No. 98/16.*

Babetski, Jan, "EU Enlargement and Endogeneity of OCA Criteria: Evidence from the CEECs", March 2003, University of Paris, mimeo.

Babetski, Jan, Laurence Boone and Mathilde Maurel, "Exchange Rate Regimes and Supply Shocks Asymmetry: The Case of the Accession Countries," *Discussion Paper No. 3408,* CEPR London 2002.

Barro, Robert and Gordon, David, "A Positive Theory of Monetary Policy in a Natural Rate Model," *Journal of Political Economy 91,* August 1983, 589-610.

Barth, Richard C. and Chorng-Huey Wong (eds.), Approaches to Exchange Rate Policy. *Choices for Developing and Transition Economies,* IMF Institute, 1994.

Baxter, Marianne and Stockman, Alan C., "Business Cycles and the Exchange-Rate Regime, Some International Evidence," *Journal of Monetary Economics 23,* 1989, 377-400.

Bayoumi Tamim, "A Formal Model of Optimum Currency Areas," International Monetary Fund, *Working Paper,* April 1994.

Bayoumi, Tamim and Barry Eichengreen, "Shocking Aspects of Monetary Unification," National Bureau of Economic Research, *Working Paper # 3949,* January 1992.

Bayomi, Tamim and Barry Eichengreen, "Is There a Conflict between EC Enlargement and European Monetary Unification," *Greek Economic Review, Vol. 15,* 1, 1993.

Bayoumi, Tamim and Barry Eichengreen, "One Money or Many? Analyzing the Prospects for Monetary Unification in Various Parts of the World," *Princeton Studies in International Finance, No.76,* September 1994.

Bayoumi, Tamim and Barry Eichengreen, "Ever Closer to Heaven? An Optimum-Currency-Area Index for European Countries," *European Economic Review 41,* 1997, 761-770.

Bayoumi, Tamim and Eswar Prasad, "Currency Unions, Economic Fluctuations and Adjustment: Some Empirical Evidence," Centre for Economic Policy Research, *Discussion Paper Series, No. 1172,* May 1995.

Bean, Charles R., "Economic and Monetary Union in Europe", Journal *of Economic Perspectives, Vol. 6,* Number 4, Fall 1992, 31-52.

Begg, David, "Monetary Policy during Transition: Progress and Pitfalls in Central and Eastern Europe," *Oxford Review of Economic Policy, vol 13,* No.2, 1997.

Begg, David, "Pegging Out: Lessons from the Czech Exchange Rate Crisis," *Birkbeck College, London and CEPR,* December 1997, mimeo.

Berger, Helge, Jan-Egbert Sturm, and Jakob de Haan, "An Empirical Investigation into Exchange Rate Regime Choice and Exchange Rate Volatility," *CESifo Working Paper,* 2000, No. 263

Berger, Helge, Henrik Jensen and Guttorm Schjelderup, "To Peg or Not to Peg? A Simple Model of Exchange Rate Regime Choice in Small Economies," *CESifo Working Papers, Working Paper No. 468,* April 2001

Berglof, Erik and Patrick Bolton, "The Great Divide and Beyond: Financial Architecture in Transition," *William Davidson Working Paper, Number 414,* December 2001.

Bini Smaghi, Lorenzo and Silvia Vori, "Rating the EU as an Optimal Currency Area," Banca d'Italia, *Discussion Paper, No. 187,* 1993

Blanchard, Olivier J. and Danny Quah, "The Dynamic Effects of Aggregate Demand and Supply Disturbances", *American Economic Review,* 1989 September, 655-673.

Blanchard, O., R. Dornbusch, P. Krugman, R. Layard, and L. Summers, Reform In Eastern Europe, *The MIT Press,* 1991.

Blanchard, Olivier, Jean and Lawrence F. Katz, "Regional Evolutions," *Brookings Papers on Economic Activity,* 1, 1992

Bofinger, Peter, "Is Europe an Optimum Currency Area?" Centre for Economic Policy Research, *Discussion Paper Series, No. 915,* February 1994.

Bofinger, Peter, Heiner Flassbeck and Lutz Hoffmann, "Orthodox Money-Based Stabilization (OMBS) versus Heterodox Exchange Rate-Based Stabilization (HERBS): The Case of Russia, The Ukraine and Kazachstan", *Economic Systems, Vol. 21, No.1,* March 1997.

Bogetic, Zeljko, "Full Dollarization: Fad or Future,?" *Challenge,* March 2000.

Bonin, John and Paul Wachtel, "Lessons from Bank Privatization in Central Europe," *Working Paper Number 245,* May 1999, William Davidson Institute, University of Michigan

Bonin, John P. and Mark E. Schaffer, "Revisiting Hungary's Bankruptcy Episode," *Working Paper Number 255,* September 1999, William Davidson Institute, University of Michigan.

Boone, L. and Mathilde Maurel, "An Optimal Currency Area Perspective of the EU Enlargement to the CEECs," CEPR London, *Discussion Paper No. 2119,* 1999

Boone, L., "Symmetry and Asymmetry of Supply and Demand Shocks in the European Union: A Dynamic Analysis," 1997, *Document de travail CEPII,* 97-03.

Bordo, Michael D. "Exchange Rate Regime Choice in Historical Perspective" *paper prepared for the Henry Thornton Lecture at the Cass Business School,* City University, London, England, March 26, 2003.

Brabant, van Jozef M. "Remaking Europe, The European Union and the Transition Economies," *Rowman and Littlefield Publishers,* 1999

Brada Josef C. and Ali M. Kutan, "The Czech Republic," in Desai, Padma, ed. Going Global. Transition from Plan to Market in the World Economy, *The MIT Press,* 1997.

Brada, Josef C. and Z. Drabek, "The Impact of Exchange Rate Regimes on the Stability of Trade Policy," *mimeo* 1998.

Broda, Christian, Uncertainty, Exchange Rate Regimes, and National Price Levels, Federal Reserve Bank of New York, *mimeo* 2002

Bruno, Michael, "Crisis, Stabilization, and Economic Reform," *Clarendon Press,* Oxford 1993.

Bruno, Michael, "High Inflation and the Nominal Anchors of an Open Economy," *Essays in International Finance, No. 183,* Department of Economics, Princeton University, June 1991.

Bubula, Andrea and Inci Otker-Robe, "The Evolution of Exchange Rate Regimes since 1990: Evidence from de Facto Policies," *International Monetary Fund,* WP02/155, September 2002

Buch, Claudia M. and Ralph P. Heinrich, "The End of the Czech Miracle," *Kiel Discussion Papers 301,* June 1997.

Buiter, Willem, H., "Macroeconomic Policy During a Transition to Monetary Union," *Centre for Economic Policy Research, No. 1222,* August 1995

Buiter, W. H., and G. Grafe, "Patching up the Pact: Some Suggestions for Enhancing Fiscal Sustainability and Macroeconomic Stability in an Enlarged European Union," *CEPR Discussion Paper, 3496,* 2002.

Burdekin, Richard C.K. and Thomas D. Willett "Designing Central Bank Arrangements to Promote Monetary Stability" in Willett, Thomas D., Richard C.K. Burdekin, Richard J. Sweeney and Clas Wihlborg, ed. "Establishing Monetary Stability in Emerging Market Economies," *Westview Press, Boulder* 1995

Calvo, Guillermo A., "On Dollarization," University of Maryland, April 1999, *mimeo.*

Calvo, Guillermo, and Carmen M. Reinhart, "Fear of Floating," *Quarterly Journal of Economics, Vol. CXVII,* No. 2, May 2002, pp. 379-408

Calvo, Guillermo A., and Frederic S. Mishkin, "The Mirage of Exchange Rate Regimes for Emerging Market Countries," *NBER Working Paper 9808,* June 2003

Canzoneri, Matthew B. and Carol Ann Rogers, "Is the European Community an Optimal Currency Area? Optimal Taxation versus the Cost of Multiple Currencies," *American Economic Review, Vol. 80,* No. 3, June 1990

Chamie, Nick, Alain DeSerres, and René Lalonde, "Optimum Currency Areas and Shock Asymmetry. A Comparison of Europe and the United States," Bank of Canada, *Working Paper 94-1,* 1994

Cohen, Benjamin, The Geography of Money, Cornell University Press 1998.

Cohen, D. and Charles Wyplosz, "The European Monetary Union: An Agnostic Evaluation," *Discussion Paper No. 306,* Centre for Economic Policy Research, London, 1989

Commission of the European Communities, "One Market, One Money," *European Economy, 44,* 1990.

Cooper, Richard, "Exchange Rate Choices," June 1999, mimeo.

Corden, Max, "The Adjustment Problem" in Krause and Salant (eds.), *European Monetary Unification and its Meaning for the United States,* Washington, Brookings, 1973, 159-184.

Coorey, S., M. Mecagni and E. Offerdal, Disinflation in Transition Economies: The Role of Relative Price Adjustments. *IMF Working Paper, 96/138,* December 1996

Coricelli, Fabrizio and Valerio Ercolani, "Cyclical and Structural Deficits on the Road to Accession: Fiscal Rules for an Enlarged European Union," Centre for Economic Policy Research, *CEPR, No. 3672,* December 2002

Corker, Robert, Craig Beaumont, Rachel van Elkan, and Dora Iakova, "Exchange Rate Regimes in Selected Advanced Transition Economies – Coping with Transition, Capital Inflows, and EU Accession," *IMF Policy Discussion Paper,* 2000, PDP/00/3

Corsetti, Giancarlo and Paolo Pesenti, "Self-Validating Optimum Currency Areas," Federal Reserve Bank of New York, May 2002.

Corsetti, Giancarlo and Paolo Pesenti, "International Dimensions of Optimal Monetary Policy," *NBER Working Paper No. 8230,* April 2001

Cukierman, Alex, "Central Bank Strategy, Credibility, and Independence Theory and Evidence *The MIT Press* 1992, Second edition 1994.

Czech National Bank Reports, various issues.

Darne, Olivier and Laetitia Ropill-Bresson, "Exchange Rate Regime Classification and Real Performances," *mimeo* 2003

Dedek, O., Echoing the European Monetary Integration in the Czech Republic, Czech National Bank, *Working Paper # 80,* 1997.

Demopoulos, George D. and Nicholas A. Yannacopoulos, "Conditions for Optimality of a Currency Area," *Open Economies Review, 10,* 1999, 289-303.

Dibooglu, Selahattin and Julius Horvath, "Optimum Currency Areas and European Monetary Unification," *Contemporary Economic Policy, 1997, Volume 15, Number 1,* 37-49

Dornbusch, Rudiger, "Inflation, Exchange Rates and Stabilization" *Essays in International Finance No. 165,* Princeton University, International Finance Section, October 1986.

Dornbusch, Rudiger, Francesco Giavazzi, "Hard Currency and Sound Credit: A Financial Agenda For Central Europe" 1998, mimeo.

Dornbusch, Rudiger, F. Sturzenegger, and Holger Wolf, "Hyperinflations: Sources and Stabilization," *Brookings Papers on Economic Activity, 2,* 1990.

Ecofin Council "Exchange rate aspects of enlargement, European economy", *Reproduced in the European Economy Supplement C, No. 1,* February 2001

Edwards, Sebastian, "Exchange Rates as Nominal Anchors," Weltwirschaftliches Archiv, 1993, *Band 129, Heft 1, 1-32.*

Edwards, Sebastian, "The Determinants of the Choice between Fixed and Flexible Exchange-rate Regimes," National Bureau of Economic Research, *Working Paper No. 5756,* 1996

Eichengreen, Barry, International Monetary Arrangements for the 21st Century, *The Brookings Institution,* D.C. 1994.

Eichengreen, Barry, "Globalizing Capital, A History of the International Monetary System," *Princeton University Press,* 1996.

European Central Bank, "The Eurosystem and the EU Enlargement Process", *ECB Monthly Bulletin,* February 2000

Fatas, Antonio, "EMU: Countries or Regions? Lessons from the EMS Experience," *European Economic Review,* 1997, 4, 743-751.

Feldstein, Martin, "Why Maastricht Will Fail," *The National Interest,* 1993, No. 32, Summer.

Feldstein, Martin, "EMU and International Conflict," *Foreign Affairs*, November-December, 1997, 60-73.

Fidrmuc, Jan, Jarko Fidrmuc and Julius Horvath, "Visegrad Economies: Growth Experience and Prospects," paper prepared for the World Bank Global Research Project, *Determinants of Economic Growth*, 2002.

Fidrmuc, Jarko and Iikka Korhonnen, "Similarity of Supply and Demand Shocks between the Euro Area and the CEECs," Austrian National Bank, mimeo 2001.Fidrmuc, Jan and Julius Horvath, "Stability of Monetary Unions: Lessons from the Break-up of Czechoslovakia," *Working Paper, University of Tilburg, CentER,* 1998.

Fidrmuc, Jan, Julius Horvath and Jarko Fidrmuc, "Stability of Monetary Unions: Lessons from the Break-up of Czechoslovakia," *Journal of Comparative Economics, Vol. 27,* No. 4, December 1999, 753-81.

Fidrmuc, Jan, Jarko Fidrmuc and Julius Horvath, Visegrad Economies: Growth Experience and Projects; May 2002, Prepared for the GDN Global Research Project: *Determinants of Economic Growth Country Study for the GDN Project*

Fidrmuc, Jarko and Iikka Korhonen, "The Euro Goes East: Implications of the 2000-2002 Economic Slowdown for Synchronisation of Business Cycles between the Euro Area and CEECs," BOFIT Discussion Papers, Bank of Finland, 2003, No. 6; *Comparative Economic Studies,* 2004, 46, pp. 45-62.

Fidrmuc, Jarko and Iikka Korhonen, "Similarity of Supply and Demand Shocks between the Euro Area and the CEECs," *BOFIT Discussion Paper 13,* Bank of Finland, Institute for Economies in Transition, Helsinki, 2001.

Fidrmuc, Jarko, "Endogeneity of the Optimum Currency Area Criteria, Intraindustry Trade, and EMU Enlargement," *Discussion Paper No. 106/2001,* Centre for Transition Economics, Katholike Universiteit, Leuven, 2001.

Fischer, Stanley, "Stability and Exchange Rate Systems in a Monetarist Model of the Balance of Payments," *in The Political Economy of Monetary Reform,* ed. By Robert Z. Aliber, Allanheld, Osmun and Co., 1977.

Fischer, Stanley, "Exchange Rates versus Money Targets in Disinflation," in Stanley Fischer, ed., *Indexing, Inflation, and Economic Policy,* MIT Press, 1986, pp. 247-262.

Fischer, Stanley, "Exchange Rate Regimes: Is the Bipolar View Correct?" *Journal of Economic Perspectives, 2001, Vol. 50,* no.2 (spring) 3-24.

Fleming, Marcus J. "On Exchange Rate Unification," *Economic Journal, Vol. 81,* 1971, 467-88.

Flood, Robert F., "Capital Mobility and the Choice of Exchange Rate System," *International Economic Review, Vol 20,* 1979, 405-16.

Flood, Robert and Peter M. Garber, " Collapsing Exchange-Rate Regimes," *Journal of International Economics,* 1984, 17, 1-13.

Flood, Robert, and Andrew Rose, "Fixing Exchange Rates: A Virtual Quest for Fundamentals," *Journal of Monetary Economics,* 1995, 36, 1, 3-37

Flood, Robert and Nancy Marion, "Perspectives on the Recent Currency Crisis Literature," November 1997, Paper presented at a Washington, DC conference honoring Robert Mundell.

Fontagne, Lionel and Michael Freudenberg, "Endogenous Symmetry of Shocks in a Monetary Union," *Open Economies Review,* 1999, 10, 263-287.

Frankel, Jeffrey, A., "No Single Currency Regime is Right for All Countries or at All Times," *mimeo* 1999.

Frankel, Jeffrey A., "Experiences of and Lessons from Exchange Rate Regimes in Emerging Economies" Harvard University, 2002, *mimeo* (August).

Frankel, Jeffrey A. and Andrew K. Rose, "The Endogeneity of the Optimum Currency Area Criteria," revised draft, 1997, *mimeo.*

Frankel, Jeffrey A., Eduardo Fajnzylber, Sergio L. Schmukler, and Luis Serven, "Verifying Exchange Rate Regimes," *Journal of Development Economics, Vol. 66,* 2001, 351-386

Fratianni, Michele, and Jurgen von Hagen, The European Monetary System and European Monetary Union, Vestview Press 1992

Frenkel, Jacob A. and Joshua Aizenman, "Aspects of the Optimal Management of Exchange Rates," *Journal of International Economics, Vol. 13,* 1982.

Frenkel, Michael and Christiane Nickel, "How Symmetric are the Shocks and the Shock Adjustment Dynamics between the Euro Area and Central and Eastern European Countries," *Working Paper No. 02/222,* International Monetary Fund, 2002.

Frenkel, Michael, Christiane Nickel and Gunter Schmidt, "Some Shocking Aspects of EMU Enlargement," Deutsche Bank Research, Research Note RN-99-4, April 1999.

Friedman, Milton (1953), The Case for Flexible Exchange Rates, in *Essays in Positive Economics,* the University of Chicago Press pp.157-203

Funke, Michael, "The Nature of Shocks in Europe and in Germany," *Economica,* 1997, 64, 461-69.

Gács, János, "Macroeconomic Developments in Hungary and the Accession Process," *Interim Report IR-00-013, IIAS,* Vienna, March 2000.

Gács, János and Georg Winckler eds. International Trade and Restructuring in Eastern Europe, *Physica-Verlag, Springer-Verlag Company* 1994.

Gandolfo, Giancarlo, International Economics II, International Monetary Theory and Open-Economy Macroeconomics, *Springer-Verlag,* Second Revised Edition, 1995.

Garber, Peter M. and Lars E. O. Svensson " The Operation and Collapse of Fixed Exchange Rate Regimes," NBER, 1994, *Working Paper No. 4971.*

Gershenkron, Alexander, *Economic Backwardness in Historical Perspective,* The Belknap Press of Harvard University Press, 1962, Third Printing 1976, Chapter 1 *Economic Backwardness in Historical Perspective,* pp. 5-30.

Ghosh, Atish R. and Holger C. Wolf, "How Many Monies? A Genetic Approach to Finding Optimum Currency Areas", National Bureau of Economic Research, 1994, July, *Working Paper # 4805.*

Ghosh, Atish R., Anne-Marie Gulde and Holger C. Wolf, Exchange Rate Regimes, Choices and Consequences, *The MIT Press,* 2002

Ghosh, Atish, Anne-Marie Gulde, Jonathan Ostry, and Holger Wolf, "Does the Nominal Exchange Rate Regime Matter?, *NBER Working Paper, No. 5874,* January 1997

Giavazzi, Francesco and Alberto Giovannini, Limiting Exchange Rate Flexibility, *The European Monetary System, MIT Press,* 1989.

Giavazzi, F., and M. Pagano, "The Advantage of Tying One's Hands: EMS Discipline and the Central Bank Credibility," *European Economic Review, 1988, Vol. 32.*

Giersch, Herbert, "On the Desirable Degree of Flexibility of Exchange Rates," *Weltwirtschaftliches Archiv,* 1973, Band 109, 191-213.

Goldberg, Linda S., "Is Optimum Currency Area Theory Irrelevant for Economies in Transition?" in R.J. Sweeney, C. Wihlborg and T.D. Willett (eds.), Exchange Rate Policies for Emerging Market Economies, *Westview Press,* 1999, 45-60.

Golinelli, Roberto and Riccardo Rovelli, "Painless Disinflation? Monetary Policy Rules in Hungary, 1991-1999" University of Bologna, *mimeo,* April 2001.

Gomulka, Stanislaw, "Policy Challenges within the (Enlarged) European Union: How to Foster Economic Convergence?", The Austrian Central Bank's Conference on Convergence and Divergence in Europe, Vienna, November 2001.

Goodhart, Charles, "Economists' Perspectives on the EMS. A Review Essay," *Journal of Monetary Economics,* 26, 1990, 471-487.

Goodhart, Charles, "The Political Economy of Monetary Union," in Peter B. Kenen (ed.), 1994, 450-505.

Goodhart, Charles, "European Monetary Integration," *European Economic Review,* 1996, 40, 1083-1090.

Grabowski, Richard and Julius Horvath, "Economic Integration in Central America and the Caribbean," *Journal of Economic Development,* 1999, Volume 24, Number 1, 121-132.

Grandes, Martin, "Southern Africa's Monetary Area: an Optimal Currency Area?" DELTA, École des Hautes Études en Sciences Sociales/École Normale Supérieure, July 2003

Grauwe, Paul de and Wim Vanhaverbeke, "Is Europe an Optimum Currency Area? Evidence from Regional Data," Centre for Economic Policy Research, *Discussion Paper Series, No. 556, 1991.*

Grauwe, Paul de, The Economics of Monetary Integration, Second Revised Edition, Oxford University Press, 1994.

Grubel, Herbert G. "The Theory of Optimum Currency Areas", *Canadian Journal of Economics,* 1970, May, 318-324.

Guitián, Manuel, "The Choice of an Exchange Rate Regime," in Barth and Wong (eds.) *Approaches to Exchange Rate Policy,* IMF Institute, 1994.

Gulde, Anne-Marie, "The Role of the Currency Board in Bulgaria's Stabilization," International Monetary Fund, Policy *Discussion Paper, 1999, PDP/99/3.*

Gylfason, Thorvaldur, "The Potential Consequences of Alternative Exchange Rate Regimes – A Study of Three Candidate Regions: Comment," 2002, Vienna, *Conference on Monetary Union,* 14-16 April

Haberler, Gottfried, "The International Monetary System: Some Recent Developments and Discussions," in Money in the International Economy, Halm (ed.), 1970.

Hagen von, Jürgen and Manfred J.M. Neumann, "Real Exchange Rates within and between Currency Areas: How Far Away Is EMU?" *Review of Economics and Statistics,* 1994 August, 236-244

Hagen von, Jürgen and Jizhong Zhou, "The Choice of Exchange Rate Regimes: an Empirical Analysis for Transition Economies," Centre for Economic Policy Research, International Macroeconomics, *Working Paper No. 3289,* 2002

Halm, George, (ed.), Approaches to Greater Flexibility of Exchange Rates: The Burgenstock Papers, Princeton University Press, 1970.

Halpern, László, and Charles Wyplosz, "Equilibrium Exchange Rates in Transition Economies," *International Monetary Staff Papers,* December 1997, pp. 430-61.

Halpern, László, and Judit Neményi, "Balance of Payments, Exchange Rates, and Competitiveness in Hungary, " in Mario I. Blejer and Marko Skreb edited, *Balance of Payments, Exchange Rates, and Competitiveness in Transition Economies,* Kluwer Academic Publishers, 1999.

Hausmann, Ricardo, Ugo Panizza, and Ernesto Stein, "Why Do Countries Float the Way They Float?" *Journal of Development Economics, Vol 66,* 2001, 387-414

Havrylyshyn O., Ivailo Izvorski, and Ron van Rooden, "Recovery and Growth in Transition Economics 1990-97: a Stylized Regression Analysis," *IMF Working Paper, 1998, WP/98/141.*

Heller, Robert, "Determinants of Exchange Rate Practices," *Journal of Money, Credit and Banking,* August 1978, 308-321.

Helpman, Elhanan, "An Exploration in the Theory of Exchange-Rate Regimes," *Journal of Political Economy, 1981, vol. 89,* No.5, 865-890.

Helpman, Elhanan and Assaf Razin, "A Comparison of Exchange Rate Regimes in the Presence of Imperfect Capital Markets, " *International Economic Review, Vol. 23,* No. 2, June 1982.

Hochreiter, Eduard "Central Banking in Economies in Transition" in Willett, Thomas D., Richard C.K. Burdekin, Richard J. Sweeney and Clas Wihlborg, ed. "Establishing Monetary Stability in Emerging Market Economies," *Westview Press, Boulder* 1995

Hochreiter, Eduard, "EU Enlargement – the Exchange Rate Policy Side – an Austrian Perspective," *CESifo Forum,* Summer 2001, 19-23, mimeo.

Horvath, Julius and Richard Grabowski, "Prospects of African Integration in Light of the Theory of Optimum Currency Areas," *Journal of Economic Integration, 1997, Volume 12,* Number 1, 1-25.

Horvath, Julius, "Supply and Demand Shocks in Europe: Large-4 EU Members, Visegrad-5 and Baltic-3 Countries, Central European University, 2000, *mimeo.*

Horvath, Julius and Jiri Jonas, "Exchange Rate Regimes in the Transition Economies, Case Study of the Czech Republic: 1990-1997," University of Bonn, Center for European Integration Studies, ZEI, *Working Paper, 1998, B 11.*

Horvath, Julius, "Currency Crisis in the Czech Republic in May 1997", *Post-Communist Economies,* 1999, *Vol. 11,* Number 3, pp. 277-298.

Horvath, Julius and Attila Ratfai, "Supply and Demand Shocks in Countries to Join the EMU," *Journal of Comparative Economics*, 2004, June, 32, pp. 202-211.

Horvath, Roman and Lubos Komarek, "Optimum Currency Area Theory: An Approach for Thinking about Monetary Integration," *Warwick Economic Research Papers, Department of Economics, No. 647,* August 2002.

Hrncir, Miroslav, "Exchange Rate Regimes for the Stages of Transition," Financial Reform in Central and Eastern Europe EC(ACE) Project No. ERB 4012 PL 900 69 Conference; Prague 3-4 September 1993.

Hrncir, Miroslav, "The Exchange Rate and Transition: The Case of the Former Czechoslovakia," in Herr, Hansjorg, Silke Tober and Andreas Westphal, ed. Macroeconomic Problems of Transformation. *Stabilization Policies and Economic Restructuring,* Edward Elgar 1994. ed. 1994, pp. 228-255.

Hrncir, Miroslav, "Economic Recovery and Foreign Exchange Rate Regime: The Case of the Czech Republic," in Gacs, Janos and Georg Winckler eds. *International Trade and Restructuring in Eastern Europe,* Physica-Verlag, Springer-Verlag Company 1994.

Hungarian Financial Supervisory Authority, "Report on the Development of the Supervised Sectors in the First Three Quarters of 2001,"

IMF Public Information Notice No. 01/47, IMF Concludes Article IV Consultation with Hungary, May 18, 2001

Ingram, James C., "Comment: The Currency Area Problem." in *Monetary Problems of the International Economy,* Robert A. Mundell and Alexander R. Swoboda (eds.), The University of Chicago Press, Chicago and London, 1969.

Ingram, James C., "Comments," in Krause and Salant (eds.), *European Monetary Unification and its Meaning for the United States,* Washington, Brookings, 1973, 184-191.

International Monetary Fund, "Czech Republic. Selected Issues." 1998

Ishiyama, Yoshihide "The Theory of Optimum Currency Areas: A Survey," *Staff Papers International Monetary Fund,* 1975, *Vol. 22,* pp.344-83.

Johnson, Harry G., "The Case for Flexible Exchange Rates, 1969," in Halm (1970), 91-111, Reprinted in Johnson, 1973.

Johnson, Harry G., Further Essays in Monetary Economics, Harvard University Press, 1973.

Kareken John, and Neil Wallace, "On the Indeterminacy of Equilibrium Exchange Rates," *The Quarterly Journal of Economics,* May 1981, pp. 207-222.

Kenen, Peter, "The Theory of Optimum Currency Areas: An Eclectic View," in Mundel and Swoboda (eds.) *Monetary Problems in the International Economy,* University of Chicago Press, 1969.

Kenen, Peter, ed. Understanding Interdependence: the Macroeconomics of the Open Economy, Princeton University Press, Princeton, New Jersey, 1994(a).

Kenęn, Peter, "Floating Exchange Rates Reconsidered," in Peter B. Kenen, Francesco Papadia, and Fabrizio Saccomanni edited, *The International Monetary System, Proceedings of a Conference Organized by the Banca d'Italia,* Cambridge University Press, 1994.

Kenen, Peter, Economic and Monetary Union in Europe, Cambridge University Press, 1995.

Kim, Sukkoo, "Economic Integration and Convergence: U.S. Regions, 1840-1987," NBER Working Paper No. 6335, 1997, December

Kindleberger, Charles P. A Financial History of Western Europe, Oxford University Press 1993.

Klaus, Vaclav, "Promoting Financial Stability in the Transition Economies of Central and Eastern Europe," in Maintaining Financial Stability in a Global Economy. A Symposium Sponsored by the Federal Reserve Bank of Kansas City, 1997.

Kocenda, Evzen, "EMU and the Accession Countries," *mimeo* 2004.

Krause,Lawrence B. and Walter S. Salant ed. European Monetary Unification and Its Meaning for the United States, The Brookings Institution, Washington, 1973.

Krugman, Paul R. "A Model of Balance-of-Payments Crises," *Journal of Money, Credit and Banking* 11(3), 1979, pp. 311-325.

Krugman, Paul, Geography and Trade, Cambridge, *MIT Press,* 1991.

Krugman, Paul, "Lessons of Massachusetts for EMU," In F. Torres and F. Giavazzi ed. Adjustment and Growth in the European Monetary Union, 1993.

Krugman, Paul, "What Do We Need to Know about the International Monetary System?" in Kenen ed. 1994

Krugman, Paul and Lance Taylor, "Contractionary Effects of Devaluation," *Journal of International Economics,* 1978, 8, August, 445-56.

Krugman Paul and Anthony Venables "Integration and the Competitiveness of Peripheral Industry." In Bliss and de Macedo, eds. *Unity with Diversity in the European Community,* Cambridge University Press, 1990, 56-75.

Krugman, Paul, "Target Zones and Exchange Rate Dynamics," *Quarterly Journal of Economics,* 56, 3, August 1991 pp. 669-682.

Krugman, Paul, "Exchange Rates in a Currency Band: a Sketch of the New Approach," in Krugman, P. and M. Miller ed. *Exchange Rate Targets and Currency Bands,* Cambridge University Press, 1992, reprinted 1995, pp. 9-14.

Kwan, Yum K. and Francis T. Lui "Hong Kong's Currency Board and Changing Monetary Regimes,", National Bureau of Economic Research, *Working Paper, 1996, #5723*

Lafrance, Robert and Pierre St-Amant, "Optimum Currency Areas: A Review of the Recent Literature," *Bank of Canada Working Paper, 1999, 99-16.*

Larain, Felipe B and Andre Velasco, " Exchange Rate Policy in Emerging Market Economies: The Case for Floating." *Essays in International Economics No.224* Dec. International Economics Section. Department of Economics. 2001, Princeton University, Princeton NJ.

Lavrac, Vladimir, "Exchange Rate Regimes of Central and Eastern European EU Candidate Countries on Their Way to EMU" *mimeo,* 2001 http://www.icegec.org/.

Levine, Ross, "Financial Development and Economic Growth," *Policy Research Working Paper,* The World Bank, Policy Research Department, October 1996

Levy-Yeyati, Eduardo and Federico Sturzeneger, "A de facto Classification of Exchange Rate Regimes: A Methodological Note," *mimeo,* 2003.

Lucas, Robert E., "Some International Evidence on Output-Inflation Tradeoffs," American *Economic Review 63,* 326–334, 1973

Lucas, Robert and Nancy Stokey, "Money and Interest in a Cash-in-Advance Economy," *Econometrica,* May 1987, 55, No. 3, 491-513.

Machlup, Fritz, A History of Thought on Economic Integration, Columbia University Press, 1977.

Masson, Paul R. and Mark P. Taylor, (eds.), Policy Issues in the Operation of Currency Areas, Cambridge University Press, 1993.

Masson, Paul R. and Mark P. Taylor, " Optimal Currency Areas: A Fresh Look at the Traditional Criteria", in Siklos (ed.), *Varieties of Monetary Reforms,* Kluwer Academic, 1994.

Masson, Paul R. and Mark P. Taylor, "Currency Unions: A Survey of the Issues," in Masson and Taylor (eds.), *Policy Issues in the Operation of Currency Unions,* Cambridge University Press, 1993, 3-51.

Masson P.R. and M.P. Taylor (1992), "Common Currency Areas and Currency Unions: An Analysis of the Issues," *CEPR Discussion Paper No. 617.*

Masson, Paul R., "Monetary and Exchange Rate Policy of Transition Economies of Central and Eastern Europe after the Launch of EMU," *IMF Policy Discussion Paper, PDP/99/5,* July 1999.

McCallum, Bennett, International Monetary Economics, Oxford University Press, 1996.

McKinnon, Ronald I., "Optimum Currency Area," 4, *American Economic Review,* 1963, September, 717-725.

McKinnon, Ronald I., "Comment" in Mundel and Swoboda (eds.), *Monetary Problems in the International Economy,* University of Chicago Press, 1969.

Mélitz, Jacques and Axel A. Weber, "The Costs/Benefits of a Common Monetary Policy in France and Germany and Possible Lessons for Monetary Union," European University Institute, Florence, Robert Schuman Centre, 1997, *Working Paper RSC No. 97/37.*

Mélitz, Jacques, "The Current Impasse in Research on Optimum Currency Areas," *European Economic Review,* 1995, 30, 492-500.

Melvin, Michael, "The Choice of and Exchange Rate System and Macroeconomic Stability," *Journal of Money, Credit and Banking, Vol. 17,* No. 4, November 1985, 467-478.

Minford, P. "Discussion of Bayoumi and Eichengreen," in Torres and Giavazzi (eds.) *Adjustment and Growth in the European Monetary Union,* Cambridge, Cambridge University Press, 1993.

Minford, Patrick, "Other People's Money: Cash-in-Advance Microfoundations for Optimal Currency Areas," *Journal of International Money and Finance,* 14 1995, 3, 427-440.

Mintz, Norman N., "Monetary Union and Economic Integration", *The Bulletin, New York University Graduate School of Business Administration, Institute of Finance, No.64,* April 1970.

Mitchell, B.R., International Historical Statistics. Europe 1750-1988, Third Edition, Stockton Press 1992.

Mkenda, Beatrice Kalinda, "Is East Africa an Optimum Currency Area?" *Working Paper No. 41,* Department of Economics, Göteborg University, April 2001.

Monetary Policy in Hungary, May 2000, Produced by staff members of the Monetary Policy Department of the National Bank of Hungary headed by György Sándor

Mongelli, Francesco Paolo, "'New' Views on the Optimum Currency Area Theory: What is EMU Telling Us," European Central Bank, Working Paper Series, April 2002, *Working Paper No. 138.*

Mundell, Robert A., "A Theory of Optimum Currency Areas," *American Economic Review,* 1961, 657-665.

Mundell, Robert A., "Comment" in Mundel and Swoboda (eds.), *Monetary Problems in the International Economy,* University of Chicago Press, 1969.

Mundell, Robert A., "Updating the Agenda for Monetary Union," in M. I. Blejer, Jacob A. Frenkel, Leonardo Leiderman, and Assaf Razin (eds.), *Optimum Currency Areas, New Analytical and Policy Developments,* International Monetary Fund, 1977, 29-48.

National Bank of Hungary, *"Quarterly Report on Inflation,"* May 2002

National Bank of Hungary, "Statement on the New System of Monetary Policy", June 12, 2001

National Bank of Hungary, "The Hungarian Banking Sector Developments in the First Half of 2000," December 2000

Nerlich, Carolin, "Exchange Rate Strategies of EU Accession Countries: Does Exchange Rate Policy Matter?", Prepared for the KOBE Research Seminar, European Central Bank, April 2002.

Neumeyer, Pablo Andres, "Currencies and the Allocation of Risk: The Welfare Effects of a Monetary Union," *American Economic Review, Vol. 88,* No.1, March 1998, 246-259.

Niehans, Jürgen, International Monetary Economics, John Hopkins University Press, 1984.

Oblath, Gábor, "Exchange Rate Policy and Real Exchange Rate Changes in Economic Transition'" in Janos Gacs and Georg Winckler eds. *International Trade and Restructuring in Eastern Europe,* Physica-Verlag, A Springer-Verlag Company 1994.

Obstfeld, Maurice and Kenneth Rogoff, "The Mirage of Fixed Exchange Rates," Journal of Economic Perspectives, 9(4), 1995, pp. 73–96.

Obstfeld, Maurice and Kenneth Rogoff, Foundations of International Macroeconomics, *The MIT Press,* 1996.

Obstfeld, Maurice, "Models of Currency Crisis with Self-fulfilling Features," *European Economic Review,* 1996, 40, pp. 1037-1047.

Obstfeld, Maurice, Logic of Currency Crises, 1994, in Springer 1995, in *"Monetary and Fiscal Policy in an Integrated Europe,"* edited by Eichengreen, Frieden and von Hagen.

Obstfeld, Maurice, "International Macroeconomics: Beyond the Mundell-Fleming Model," National Bureau of Economic Research, *Working Paper 8369,* July 2001

Obstfeld, Maurice and Kenneth Rogoff, "New Directions for Stochastic Open Economy Models," *Journal of International Economics, Vol. L,* February 2000, pp. 117-153

OECD Economic Outlook, Chapter VII. "Enhancing Income Convergence in Central Europe after EU Accession," 2004

Orlowski, Lucjan T., „Monetary Convergence of the EU Candidates to the Euro: A Theoretical Framework and Policy Implications," Zentrum für Europäische Integrationsforschung, Bonn, *Working Paper B25,* 2001.

Padoa-Schioppa, Tommaso, "Remarks at the High Level Seminar with the EU-Candidate Countries," Press Division, European Central Bank, http://www.ecb.int/key/00/sp001221.htm, December 2000

Polak, Jacques J. "Convertibility: An Indispensable Element in the Transition Process," in Williamson ed. 1991.21-30.

Poole, William, "Optimal Choice of Monetary Policy Instruments in a Simple Stochastic Macro Model," *Quarterly Journal of Economics, Vol. 84,* May 1970.

Presley, John R. and Geoffrey E.J. Dennis, Currency Areas, Theory and Practice, *MacMillan Press,* 1976.

Puhani, Patrick A., "Labour Mobility – An Adjustment Mechanism in Euroland? Empirical Evidence for Western Germany, France, and Italy," *Discussion Paper No. 34,* March 1999, IZA, Bonn.

Reinhart, Carmen M. and Kenneth S. Rogoff, "The Modern History of Exchange Rate Arrangements: a Reintepretation," International Monetary Fund, *mimeo version* March 3, 2003

Reinhart, Carmen M. and Kenneth S. Rogoff, "The Modern History of Exchange Rate Arrangements: A Reinterpretation," National Bureau of Economic Research, June 2002, *Working Paper 8963*

Ricci, L., "A Model of an Optimum Currency Area," International Monetary Fund, 1997, *Working Paper 97/76.*

Rose, Andrew K., "After the Deluge: Do Fixed Exchange Rates Allow Inter-Temporal Volatility Trade-Offs?" 1995, *CEPR Discussion Paper 1240.*

Rose, Andrew K., "One Money, One Market: Estimating the Effect of Common Currencies on Trade," University of Berkeley, Haas School of Business, February 2000, *mimeo.*

Rostowski, Jacek (2001a), "The Eastern Enlargement of the EU and the Case for Unilateral Euroization," *mimeo*

Rostowski, Jacek, (2001b), "Why Unilateral Euroization Makes Sense for (Some) Applicant Countries - a Response, with Particular Reference to Poland," *mimeo*

Rostowski, Jacek, "Does the Existence of the Euro Require Further Political Integration of EMU Members," 2000, *mimeo*

Salant, Walter S., "Discussion" in Krause and Salant (eds.), *European Monetary Unification and its Meaning for the United States,* Washington, Brookings, 1973, 201-202.

Salant, Steve and D. Henderson, "Market Anticipation of Government Policies and the Price of Gold" *Journal of Political Economy,* August 1978

Schumpeter, Joseph A., History of Economic Analysis, New York, Oxford University Press 1954.

Siklos, Pierre and Istvan Abel "Fiscal and Monetary Policies in the Transition: Searching for the Credit Crunch" in Willett, Thomas D., Richard C.K. Burdekin, Richard J. Sweeney and Clas Wihlborg, ed. *"Establishing Monetary Stability in Emerging Market Economies,"* Westview Press, Boulder 1995

Siklos, Pierre L. and István Ábel, "Is Hungary Ready for Inflation Targeting?" *mimeo 2002,* forthcoming in Economic Systems.

Siklos, Pierre L. (ed.), Varieties of Monetary Reforms: Lessons and Experiences on the Road to Monetary Union, 1994, Kluwer Academic Publishers.

Summers, R. and Heston, A. "The Penn World Table (Mark 5): An Expanded Set of International Comparisons, 1950-1988," *Quarterly Journal of Economics 106/2,* May, 1991, pp. 327-68.

Surányi György, and János Vincze, "Inflation in Hungary, 1990-97," in Carlo Cottarelli and György Szapáry edited Moderate Inflation. *The Experience of Transition Economies, International Monetary Fund and National Bank of Hungary,* 1998.

Sweeney, Richard, Clas G. Wihlborg, and Thomas D. Willett (eds.), Exchange Rate Policies for Emerging Market Economies, Westview Press, 1999.

Swoboda, Alexander, "Robert Mundell and the Theoretical Foundation for the European Monetary Union," *Views and Commentaries,* International Monetary Fund, December, 1999, www.imf.org /external/np/vc/1999/121399.htm

Szapáry, György and Jakab M. Zoltán, "A csúszó leértékelés tapasztalatai Magyarországon," (Hungarian Experience with the Crawling Peg Regime), *Közgazdasági Szemle,* 1998, October, pp. 877-905.

Szapáry, György, „Banking Sector Reform in Hungary: Lessons Learned, Current Trends and Prospects," National Bank of Hungary, *Working Paper 2001/5,* December 2001.

Szapáry, György, "Transition Countries' Choice of Exchange Rate in the Run-Up to EMU Membership," *Finance and Development,* June 2001, Volume 38, Number 2.

Tang, Helena, Edda Zoli and Irina Klytchnikova, "Banking Crises in Transition Countries: Fiscal Costs and Related Issues," World Bank, 2000.

Tavlas, George S., "The 'New' Theory of Optimum Currency Areas", *The World Economy, Vol. 16,* 1993, 663-685.

Tower, E. and T. D. Willett, "The Theory of Optimum Currency Areas and Exchange-Rate Flexibility: A More General Framework," *Special Papers in International Economics 11,* Princeton University, 1976.

United Nations Economic Commission for Europe, Economic Survey of Europe, 2003/1.

Várhegyi Éva, "Hungary's Experience in the Crawling Peg Regime: Benefits and Costs," Financial Research Ltd. Budapest, Paper presented in ACE conference, 21 September 2001 Vienna.

Várhegyi Éva, "Külföldi tulajdon a magyar bankrendszerben," [Foreign Ownership in Hungarian Banking System,], *Közgazdasági Szemle,* 2001, July-August, pp. 581-598.

Várhegyi Éva, "Hungarian Banking Sectors after Privatization," *Central European Banker,* February 1999, pp. 5-12.

Vaubel, Roland, "Currency Unification, Currency Competition, and the Private ECU: Second Thoughts," in *International and European Monetary Systems,* Emil-Maria Claassen (ed.), Praeger, 1990.

Vaubel, Roland, "The Centralization of Western Europe, The Common Market, Political Integration, and Democracy," Institute of Economic Affairs, *Hobart Paper* 127, 1995.

Velde, Francois R. and Marcelo Veracierto, "Dollarization in Argentina," Federal Reserve Bank of Chicago, *Economic Perspectives,* 2000, 24-35.

Vinals, Jose, "European Monetary Integration: A Narrow or a Wide EMU?" *European Economic Review,* 1996, 40, 1103-1109

Vincze, János, "Financial Stability, Monetary Policy and Integration: Policy Choices for Transition Economies," National Bank of Hungary, *Working Paper, 2001/4,* December 2001.

Wagner, Nancy and Dora Iakova, "Financial Sector Evolution in the Central European Economies: Challenges in Supporting Macroeconomic Stability and Sustainable Growth," International Monetary Fund, *Working Paper, 2001, WP/01/141.*

Wallace, Neil, "Why Markets in Foreign Exchange are Different from Other Markets," Federal Reserve Bank of Minneapolis, *Quarterly Review,* 1979, 3, 1-17

Walsh, Carl E., Monetary Theory and Policy, *The MIT Press,* 1998.

Walters, Alan, "Currency Boards" New Palgrave Money edited by Eatwell, Milgate and Newman, W.W. Norton, 1989, pp. 109-114.

Weber, Axel A., "EMU and Asymmetries and Adjustment Problems in the EMS: Some Empirical Evidence," CEPR, Centre for Economic Policy Research, 1990, *Discussion Paper No. 448.*

Whitt, Joseph A. Jr., "European Monetary Union: Evidence from Structural VARs", Federal Reserve Bank of Atlanta, *Working Paper Series,* 1995-1, March 1995.

Willett D. Thomas, "Some Often Neglected Aspects of the Political Economy of European Monetary Integration in Abegaz et al. (eds.), *The Challenge of European Integration,* Westview Press, 1994.

Willett, D. Thomas and Clas Wihlborg, "The Relevance of the Optimum Currency Area Approach for Exchange Rate Policies in Emerging Market Economies," in Sweeney, Wihlborg, and Willett (eds.), 1999, 61-79.

Willett, D. Thomas, "The OCA Approach to Exchange Rate Regimes: A Perspective on Recent Developments," prepared for conference on "Should Canada and the US Adopt a Common Currency," Western Washington University, April 1999, *mimeo version* 2001.

Willett, Thomas D. "Guidelines for Constructing Monetary Constitutions" in Willet, Burdekin, Sweeney and Wihlborg edited (1995)

Willett, Thomas D., Richard C.K. Burdekin, Richard J. Sweeney and Clas Wihlborg, ed. "Establishing Monetary Stability in Emerging Market Economies," *Westview Press,* Boulder 1995

Williamson, John, ed. Currency Convertibility in Eastern Europe, Institute for International Economics, Washington, DC. September 1991.

Williamson, John, Exchange Rate Regimes for Emerging Markets: Reviving the Intermediate Option, Institute for International Economics, Washington, 2000

Wojczik, Cezary, (2000), "A Critical Review of Unilateral Euroization Proposals: The Case of Poland," Austrian Central Bank, Transition, 2000:2, pp. 48-76

Yuen, Hazel, "Is Asia an Optimum Currency Area? 'Shocking' Aspects of Output Fluctuations in East Asia," Department of Economics, National University of Singapore, August 2000, *mimeo.*

INDEX

E

I

J

K

L

M

N

O

P

R

S

T

U

V

W

Y